Dymphna Byrne is a freelance journalist who for the last seven years has specialized in camping. During her career she has been on the staff of *Good Housekeeping, House Beautiful* and *Woman*, and has contributed to *The Daily Telegraph, The Guardian, The Sunday Times* and *The Observer*. She is a member of the Guild of Travel Writers and has broadcast on *Woman's Hour*. Her enthusiasm for comfortable camping dates from the time she and her husband first started taking their three sons on holidays, and this book is the result of her experiences.

CAMPING
In Comfort

Dymphna Byrne

Hamlyn Paperbacks

CAMPING IN COMFORT
ISBN 0 600 20526 6

First published in Great Britain 1983
by Hamlyn Paperbacks

Hamlyn Paperbacks are published by
The Hamlyn Publishing Group Ltd,
Astronaut House, Feltham,
Middlesex, England

Reproduced, printed and bound in Great Britain by
Hazell Watson & Viney Ltd, Aylesbury, Bucks

Contents

Preface

This book is for my husband Joe and our sons William, James and Charles with love, affection and thanks for a decade of memorable camping holidays.

It is also for my friend and neighbour Ella Gilday, whose moral support was as welcome as her practical help with research and typing. I would like to thank Jerry Johns of the Midlands region of the AA, Maggie Parsons, former associate editor of *Drive & Trail*, and John Lloyd, editor of *Practical Camper* for their help with background material. I would also like to acknowledge all the help given by AA staff at Basingstoke and by the London-based tourist offices of the countries mentioned and to thank particularly Pauline Hallam of the French Government Tourist Office and Annette Brown, formerly of the English Tourist Board. Then there are the equipment manufacturers, ferry companies, rent-a-tent organizations, map-makers, everyone who kept me supplied with a stream of facts and figures: my thanks to all of them for their patience with my queries and for the promptness of most of their replies.

As this is the first book of its kind to be compiled I apologise for any errors that may have crept in and hope that if any readers have relevant material that might be included in a possible revised version they will forward it to the publishers.

Finally, as this first venture into writing books as opposed to short articles proved more alarming than I had anticipated, I would like to thank Nina Shandloff of Hamlyn for her calmness in the face of my mounting panic and her editor, Ruth Baldwin, for the very clear-sighted way in which she put the final shape to the book.

Prices and costings

In order to help give a general idea of the cost of camping, I have noted prices on a number of occasions, particularly where equipment is concerned and sometimes for package tent holidays offered by holiday organizations not normally associated with camping. These figures are meant only as guidelines to help give an overall picture. The prices of equipment were checked in 1982, but they could rise for 1983, while there might be a ten percent increase in the charges made by holiday companies for camping packages.

The summer of 1982 saw a number of changes in the rent-a-tent market. By 1983 there may have been mergers, and one or two names may fail to resurface after the winter break.

Introduction

At last the British have realized that camping can be comfortable and enjoyable as well as economical. So comfort just as much as cost accounts for the rapid rise in popularity of camping holidays over the past decade. These days the majority of campers, who come from all social backgrounds, all income brackets and all age groups, camp because they want to rather than for economic reasons, as was shown by a survey carried out in this country by the Camping Club of Great Britain and Ireland, the oldest camping club in the world.

Not only has equipment improved enormously during the past ten years, but nowadays camp sites often have better facilities than many tourist hotels. Moreover, campers with their own equipment (and even 'rent-a-tent' campers in the low season when 'tent hopping' is permitted) enjoy a freedom denied the average holiday-maker. The main disadvantage of camping – having occasionally to put up with bad weather – is more than offset by the flexibility this type of holiday offers.

Comfort

Whether you take your own gear or rent a tent, careful planning is the key to comfortable camping; and this means organizing the holiday at least six months ahead.

Rent-a-tent companies get their brochures out around Christmas; so if you plan to camp this way, particularly if you have to go during the school holidays, there is no excuse for not booking early and getting the site you want rather than having to put up with what is left, which can happen if you leave booking until as late as Easter.

Those with their own equipment, or planning to buy it, have to think just as far ahead. Used gear has to be checked and new equipment bought (autumn and winter sales are good for this), camp sites reserved if necessary and, if you plan to go abroad, a ferry crossing booked. Routes must be worked out, and those going to Europe have to get documentation in order. All these points are covered in detail in Chapter 4.

The fact that some four million Britons now camp, at home or abroad, means that both rent-a-tent companies and equipment manufacturers are doing all they can to woo this increasing market. Rent-a-tent companies now offer any number of comfortable embellishments to induce the would-be camper to book with them: anything from sunshades on Mediterranean sites to 'proper' beds in the secondary as well as the master bedrooms and refrigerators in the kitchen. How to find the most suitable company for your holiday is discussed in Chapter 2.

On the equipment side, imaginative tent manufacturers have added straight-sided kitchen extensions to tents, an innovation which makes life much easier for the cook, some provide a choice of steel or light alloy tent frame and, in a bid to make putting up the the tent easier and to get away from the traditional rectangular shape, a number of manufacturers have introduced new designs. Nowadays there are igloo tents, mushroom tents, hexagonal tents and some very futuristic shapes from the United States that look more eye-catching than comfortable.

Ancillary equipment has improved too. There is now a self-inflating bed which gets rid of the tedium of pumping up, there are bright fluorescent lights that run off the car battery, safe and warm catalytic heaters, portable refrigerators that run off either gas or electricity and a good selection of barbecues and non-stick griddles to widen the scope of camp cooking. How to make the best choice when buying equipment is dealt with in Chapter 1.

Cost

Since the growth of rent-a-tent holidays, where people book a fully furnished tent just as they would a holiday house, the number of those taking such a holiday and using their own car has risen considerably. There has also been a rise in the number of people taking coach-based and fly/camp holidays.

But before you rush out to book such a holiday or spend the family savings on equipment, remember that camping is not all that cheap. It does, however, cost a lot less than many other holiday choices available. Even staying at home and making daily excursions with the occasional meal out soon mounts up.

On the rent-a-tent side it was generally reckoned in 1982 that an average family – mother, father and two children – spent in the order of £400 on a self-drive two week high season package using a short sea crossing. Some companies' prices were less, others' more, with low season packages working out at around £250 for a two week holiday for a family of four.

It is harder to work out an average price for a family of four on a coach-based camping holiday, mainly because there is so much variation in what is included: some charge for cooking packs, others do not, some include insurance, others do not, and so on.

Although both types of package are discussed in Chapter 2

individual prices are not given. This is because these, which are linked to the prices being charged by camp site proprietors and ferry operators, cannot be fixed until just before the brochure is printed. You will have to write off for individual brochures to get an exact price comparison. Generally speaking most companies expect prices to rise annually by about 10 percent.

Bear in mind when calculating the cost of a holiday that self-drive rent-a-tent campers will have to include petrol. It can cost in the order of £130 for the return drive from the French ports to the Mediterranean, including petrol and motorway tolls. The cost of driving is part of the package in a coach-based holiday.

All campers are self-caterers, although some coach companies do include continental breakfasts in their charges. Even though the cost of self-catering is partly offset by the amount of money that would have been spent at home, it nevertheless costs more to eat on holiday, so allow for this. Then there is pocket money, for adults as well as children, entrance fees for museums and other places of interest and money for perhaps the occasional meal out. It is perfectly possible for a camping package with a basic price of £400 to almost double when every other expenditure has been taken into consideration. With the high cost of petrol a family of four on a self-drive camping rent-a-tent package to, say, Greece, Italy or Spain could find their holiday costing in the order of £1,000, particularly if three rather than two weeks are taken.

Those owning their own equipment and booking their own camp sites certainly pay less than those on camping packages once the capital outlay of buying the gear has been offset. As tents, the biggest piece of equipment, vary so much in price – anything from just over £150 to over £700 – for a family-sized model, it is hard to put an exact figure on the cost of equipping a family of four. A budget package could cost in the region of £300–£400, an average package perhaps between £500 and £650 with a luxury package going well over £1,000. Individual items, their suitability and approximate cost are dealt with in Chapter 1. Equipment costs are generally reckoned to be recovered over the first three or four years of camping. With camp site fees averaging out at around £1 per person per night the equipment starts paying for itself the first time it is used. The big plus point with owning your own equipment is that it can be used at weekends and not just for the annual holiday.

Flexibility and freedom

Freedom and flexibility are the main reasons given by those who camp for pleasure rather than for economic reasons: people who could quite easily afford a hotel or villa holiday, those whose children have grown up, but who still prefer the casual life of the camp site, or those who just do not like the thought of a package hotel holiday. Even renting a tent can be flexible, with a number of companies allowing holidays to start on any day of the week and encouraging campers to stay at two or three sites, although during the high season there is usually a minimum stay on any one site of five to seven days.

Those with their own gear have maximum flexibility, being able to move on when they please, stay as long as they like and, if the weather turns bad, being able to dodge the worst of the rain. The point about camping with your own gear, particularly if you have not reserved a pitch, is that if the holiday is not proving a success you can cut your losses and return home. This simply cannot be done with a hotel package holiday, and with the cost of rented tents and apartments most people feel that, however badly things are going, they cannot just leave after four days if they have paid a fortnight's rent in advance.

Freedom in camping, whether renting or using your own gear, comes in having complete control over what you do, what you wear and what and when you eat. There are very few rules on camp sites; those that do exist mainly concern silence at night, not making a nuisance of yourself during the day and driving slowly and quietly through the site grounds. The freedom to do what you like, wear what you please and eat just when you feel like it makes a strong appeal to many more than just the young and adventurous.

People mix
One of the pleasures of camping is that you get a far greater mix of people than on any other type of holiday, though to a certain extent the kind of people you meet will be determined by the sort of package or site you choose. Young unmarrieds, who enjoy a lively social life, go for camps close to or in the centre of big, bustling resorts. Families often make for areas where man-made entertainments are not so much in evidence and where peace, tranquillity and agreeable surroundings are the main attraction.

Nowadays the camp sites of Europe ring with the sound of English voices as the owners, complaining of the high cost of living at home, stir the ratatouille or de-cap the plonk. On most camp sites you will find, if you have any means of identifying them in the universal dress of shirts, sandals and shorts, lawyers, factory hands, doctors, shop-floor workers, people who work in banks, shops, schools or offices, people who work for the government, for multinationals or for themselves, and perhaps even the occasional bishop, cabinet minister or peer.

On the big international sites you will meet campers from all over Europe, although probably mainly from France, Germany and Holland, and even if you do not speak their language you will get on well together. Tents, like air-raid shelters, bring out the best in people.

It is hardly surprising that comfort and relaxation have replaced economic necessity as the main reason why so many people of widely differing backgrounds camp. A quick glance round any good European site shows that Ferraris and Mercedes are as common as Fiats and Minis and that some of the big continental tents put up for the whole season are as large and as lavish as the pavilions of medieval kings. However, they are always furnished with an eye to modern comfort and have powerful cookers, capacious refrigerators, comfortable chairs, radio and television sets, almost wall-to-wall carpeting and very often that final symbol of suburbia, net curtains.

On the continent camping has never had the impoverished and jokey image it enjoyed here for so long; more than once I have been struck by the similarity between a comfortable, well run site and a prosperous suburban housing estate. On some sites you can even tell when it is Sunday, though more for the car washing activities than the religious ceremonies that take place.

Special interest holidays

Rest and relaxation, sand and sunshine, a change from domestic duties or work routine, a way of trying a new kind of holiday – there are many reasons why people go camping. One reason that probably does not get the attention it deserves is the opportunity camping gives people to have comparatively low-cost holidays in or on the outskirts of European towns and cities. With a camp site as a base it is very easy to visit museums, art galleries, cathedrals, markets, shops, parks and zoos – all the attractions that cities have to offer. It is just a different approach to a camping holiday. Most of the major cities of Europe have sites either in the centre or close to good means of transport on the outskirts. Such camps are obviously not as picturesque nor as tranquil as those remote inland sites, but they generally have excellent facilities.

Inland country sites are often near towns of historic, cultural or architectural interest, and even seaside camps can be surprisingly close to interesting towns, areas of outstanding natural beauty or even some unusual man-made industry. For example, the famous perfume fields of Grasse are not far behind the coastal resorts of the Riviera, the Camargue is close to the beaches of the western Mediterranean, while the historic and ancient towns of Orange,

Nîmes and Avignon could be visited *en route* for Argelès or any of the fairly new resorts on that particular stretch of the Mediterranean. Camping holidays can tie in with special interests such as sailing, fishing, photography, painting, bird-watching or an interest in natural history or architecture. In fact one enterprising rent-a-tent company, Canvas Holidays, began linking special interests to some of its low season holidays in 1982; more of that in Chapter 2.

The point is to see camping in a much wider context than just staying on one site, or possibly even two, and spending all day on the beach. Find out all you can about the area before you go – this applies as much to Britain as to the continent. If you can manage to get there before the holiday rush (that is in May or June) the public library should have a good supply of source material.

However, there are some neat and not too expensive guides on sale that give excellent background information; a list of some of these will be found in the bibliography at the end of the book.

Who goes camping?

Just about everyone camps, from foot-loose teenagers to retired couples, families, single people, friends in pairs or in groups, husbands whose wives do not like camping taking the children, wives whose husbands cannot get a long summer break spending up to a month on a site with the children, single parent families. The only combination that is not looked on with favour by site proprietors, both here and on the continent, is groups of young men on their own. In fact some sites actually state that they will not accept parties of single people.

On the family side couples with babies and toddlers may find a rent-a-tent holiday more satisfactory than using their own equipment. For one thing such a holiday leaves the car boot free for all the gear so essential in the early years of childhood. Such families should check to see if a cot can be supplied and if a baby-sitting service is available. Couples who miss the freedom of using their own gear can always revert when the children are older. This can work in reverse, however. Worn out by years of careful car packing and with backs damaged by heaving awkward shapes on to roof racks, some older parents have either joyously sold all their gear or passed it on to energetic children and taken firmly to permanent renting. This is not advisable if money is a consideration – it is more expensive to continue to rent long-term than to keep on using your own equipment.

The complete informality of a camp site is a boon to parents, both when children are small and when they start roaming round on their own. If the right site has been chosen (this is dealt with in

Chapter 3) there will be adequate clothes washing facilities. Home rest patterns need not be changed as most family sites, particularly those near the coast where there is a daily exodus to the beach, are reasonably quiet. Feed times and eating habits can stay the same, and familiar food brought from home if necessary. A bonus spin-off is that, when parents are relaxed, both babies and children, sensitive to atmosphere, can sometimes be easier to handle than at home when a busy domestic routine can build up tensions.

Teenagers thrive on camping. They are much more likely to go on family holidays when they are under canvas than they are to strike off on their own as they are inclined to try to do when 'conventional' holidays are on the cards. It is easy for young people to make friends in the informal atmosphere of a camp site while evenings spent at the camp-site bar or disco are far less disturbing to parents than solo jaunts by teenagers into town.

However, camping is by no means dominated by youth. Plenty of people without children, whose children have grown up or couples who have retired go camping, particularly during the low season. Even the Mediterranean can be tranquil, as well as beautifully warm, in June and September. Prices are lower then, the shops less crowded, the traffic jams reduced to a minimum and the whole tenor of life much slower and in many ways more agreeable than in high summer. In the low season it becomes possible to see that beaches are made of sand not people.

So all the ingredients are there: it is up to you to put them together in such a way that you make sure you are camping in comfort.

1
Choosing and Buying Equipment

Buying equipment for a family of four can cost anything from £300 to over £800. The tent is the most expensive item in the pack as well as the one with the biggest price range: a family-sized tent can cost as little as £150 for a 'budget' model or well over £600 for a luxury version (more like a canvas bungalow than a tent). Even so, if the family is intending to take camping holidays for more than two or three years running, it makes sense to buy equipment. Despite the fact that freedom and flexibility now rate over economy – if only just – when it comes to camping, cost is still important to many people and when the capital investment has been laid off – generally after three years – going on holiday with one's own gear is by far the cheapest way to camp. At the time of writing, the average car-based two-week rent-a-tent holiday for a family of four in the high season, taking a short sea crossing to the continent, costs around £400. A family with its own equipment, also making a short sea crossing and spending an average of about £5 a night on camp site fees, would spend between £230 to £250 on a fortnight's holiday. Obviously the cost of food and petrol would have to be added to both sets of figures. They are quoted only to show that the recouping of money invested in camping gear begins the very first year.

Owning one's own gear also gives great flexibility as to time and place in camping. When the equipment is to hand it is possible to spend a weekend camping in this country with little or no planning, while even an unplanned dash over to France is feasible once in a while – it is just a case of getting the tent out and driving to the coast, assuming that you do not live too far from one of the Channel ports. When the weather steadies on a Friday night it is quite a thrill to decide suddenly to go camping for the weekend. The psychological boost of an unexpected break is very great and well worth any minor hiccups it causes in the domestic routine.

Another advantage of owning your own equipment is that you can range all over Europe. The majority of companies offering rent-a-tent holidays are concentrated in France, mostly around the Brittany and Mediterranean coasts, though some are now venturing inland, and a number are providing holidays in Italy, Switzerland, Austria and Spain. However, with your own equipment you can really get off the beaten track and find uncrowded sites often known to continental campers but not so well patronized by the British.

Buying from a shop

There is such a bewildering display of equipment on show at most camping shops that it is hardly surprising that many people need advice. Even old hands like to discuss purchases before reinvesting, particularly in a new tent. Designs change, new materials are introduced, safety standards are raised and new products brought in so stock is never static. That is why it is so important, particularly if you are a first-time camper, to find a store where some or preferably all of the staff actually camp. You will probably do best by going to a shop that is open throughout the year. During the summer a number of garden centres open a camping area as an added attraction, but all too often the staff know very little about camping products, so do check to see that you are buying from an informed sales person.

As well as finding a store that has experienced staff, look for one that has a reputation to keep up. A store with good standing will not sell you inadequate equipment and, what is more, it will be prepared to give you both after-sales service and the opportunity of part-exchange should you decide to up-date your equipment later. After-sales service is important, for tents can get damaged, and repairing a torn mud wall, for example, is far less expensive than buying a new tent.

Always try to get to a camping store midweek, particularly if you want advice. By the time the family's needs have been assessed and two or three different kinds of tent have been inspected, along with all the rest of the equipment, half a morning or a whole afternoon has gone. This kind of service just is not possible at weekends when shops are busier. Remember too that it is better to start looking at equipment in the early spring rather than the summer, and if you are really well organized begin your search in the autumn before you intend to start camping. At that time there are often bargains to be had as stores sell off equipment, particularly tents, rather than storing them for the winter. Traditionally the new season's camping gear goes on display at the beginning of March.

Mail order

Even if you do not intend to buy much by mail order, it is worth sending away for both of the main camping catalogues. These come out around March and April and are produced by Caseys and Scout Shops Ltd (see page 38 for addresses). The catalogues, which sell the whole range of camping equipment from tents to toilets, are valuable for two reasons. First, they give purchasers, whether they intend to buy by post or from a shop, a chance to see at their leisure, at home, what is available. First-time buyers particularly have a

15

much better idea of what they want when they go to a camping store if they have read a catalogue carefully beforehand. Second, the catalogue companies buy in bulk and, by cutting out the middle man, can offer equipment at very competitive prices.

When buying by post, however, do remember to check the carriage charges as they vary from company to company, though there are often concessions. Last year, for example, one mail order firm was dropping carriage charges on orders over a certain amount, but another was giving discount vouchers and all were offering credit facilities for hire-purchase agreements.

If you plan to buy locally, do not make the mistake of driving from shop to shop comparing prices: you will end up spending more on petrol than you save on camping equipment. Armed with the reference number, model, colour and size of your intended purchase, telephone round.

Mail order catalogues giving the name of equipment manufacturers are most useful, as these enable you to make a reasonably accurate comparison with local prices. Catalogues providing plenty of description are particularly helpful, explaining for example whether a chair frame is steel or aluminium alloy and whether the cover is canvas or nylon, whether a lantern has automatic ignition, what the weight of a sleeping bag is, the composition of the lining and so on.

The advantages of buying tents by mail order, however, are doubtful. Obviously those living in the country or far away from camping shops have no option, but they would be advised to act as follows: read the catalogue carefully, taking note of the type of canvas used in the tent, whether the frame is steel or alloy, if any accessories such as a roof liner or hanging wardrobe are included, what the weight of the tent is and how many bags make up the pack. Get the tent up as soon as it arrives and make sure that it tallies exactly with the description in the catalogue. If it does not, complain immediately: mail order companies, like shops, have a reputation to maintain.

Incidentally, both mail order companies also sell direct to the public – Caseys has seven indoor branches as well as selling through a number of garden centres during the summer months. There are at least twenty Scout Shops, known as Camping and Outdoor Centres, in various parts of the country.

Finally, that name synonymous with quality in camping and outdoor equipment for well over a hundred years – Blacks – is still around, but in various guises. Blacks of Greenock still exists as a manufacturer and wholesaler of camping equipment supplying stockists all over the country. This company issues an annual catalogue which, although it includes frame tents and camping accessories, is aimed more at the backpacker than the family camper. Blacks Camping and Leisure, now part of the Gailey organization, produces a yearly catalogue more suited to the family camper, which is obtainable from Gailey showrooms. (For the address of your nearest showroom contact the head office at the address given on page 39.) There are twenty-three Gailey camping and leisure shops in England and three in Scotland, not to be confused with the Gailey caravan and leisure showcentres (where you will not find any tents).

How to buy

Bear in mind that although camping provides relatively cheap holidays it is never worth economizing when buying the basic equipment. It really is no good at all going to the nearest discount house and asking for the cheapest tent, sleeping gear, stoves and so on. Do that and you deserve all that will most assuredly go wrong. If the family is taking up camping to avoid the cost of accommodation in hotels or holiday houses, it is false economy to try to cut costs on the equipment that is going to make all the difference between sleeping comfortably under canvas – and it is perfectly possible to be as comfortable under canvas as under concrete – and experiencing endless miserable nights. Above all, do not skimp when buying the tent and the bedding: these two items must be the best the budget can stand.

Do not buy everything at once. Get the basics – tent, sleeping gear, a cooker and something to stand it on, and possibly a table and a lantern – and then go off for a weekend's camping to discover what else you need. If you already have lightweight garden chairs, take these along to find out if they are suitable. People differ so much in what they consider to be essential that it is impossible to give a list longer than the basics above. A fiend for neatness might consider a tent tidy essential, while someone else would consider such an item a waste of £6 or so; a family keen on cooking might rate a gas-fired barbecue above a strip light; and so on.

Taking a trial weekend is useful from another point of view too. With any luck there should be some rain which will 'weather' the tent: new canvas needs a few soakings to make the fabric close up. The first time it rains on a new tent a fine spray will probably come through. This is quite normal, and the water will soon stop coming in. If you are unfortunate enough to get only good weather on your first excursion, put the tent up in a garden when rain is forecast – this is preferable to hosing the tent down as jets of water can be a little too fierce for a new tent.

Another good reason for taking equipment away on a trial weekend is to get some practice at pitching the tent. This can be dishearteningly slow at first, but as you learn to recognize the various parts of the frame you will be able to do the job more quickly. Remember to note the way in which the tent is folded: some people find that getting the tent back in its bag is almost as difficult as putting it up.

First, find a pitch as flat as possible and not too close to trees. Apart from casting too much shade, trees can disgorge torrents of water after rain and certain varieties can leak sap on to the tent. There is also the hazard of bird droppings and – though fortunately this is rare – broken branches falling on the tent. Clear the pitch of sharp stones that could cut the groundsheet and take a look at the trees to check the direction of the prevailing wind so that you can face the tent door away from it. The usual practice is to assemble the frame and leave it resting on its 'knees' while the canvas is put in place. Today's tents mostly have spring-loaded poles which makes the assembly of the frame much easier than it was. To speed up the process, sort the poles out, like with like, so that each section is readily identifiable – foot poles in one pile, roof sections in another, and so on. Once the frame is assembled, roll the canvas across it from end to end making sure that the tent is not inside out and the door is facing the way you intended. Once the canvas is square with the roof, lift the tent to its full height; it helps enormously in this operation if there can be four people helping, one at each corner. If there is any hint of wind peg the guy ropes down loosely before lifting the tent into its final position. A tent can very easily be damaged once wind gets inside an un-pegged canvas. Before finally pegging out the tent make sure that all the zips are closed otherwise the tension will be wrong. Once the tent is approximately pegged out tie the tapes on the inside of the canvas to the frame, but not to the triangular support brackets in the corners of the frame. Getting the final tension right is a process of adjustment, repositioning pegs, either farther away from or closer to the canvas, until the tent is firmly anchored, and there is no undue stress on the guys, the rubbers, the canvas or the zips. Two people, armed with a mallet apiece, speed this process up. When pegging the canvas down, as opposed to the guy ropes, start with the corners of the tent, moving the legs of the frame, if necessary, so that they fit neatly into the corner seams of the tent. Ideally, pegs should be driven into the ground as deep as possible and should make a right angle with the rubber loops or guys. In the case of tents with vertical walls, aim for an angle of 40-45 degrees.

The inner tents can then either be hung from the frame and pegged out, or pegged out before being attached to the frame. You may find the latter method easier as it avoids the necessity of crawling in the narrow space between the inner tent and the outer canvas to insert the pegs correctly. Finally, peg the groundsheet down in the living area of the tent.

Always check to see that nothing sharp leans or presses against the canvas as this can cause leaks in wet weather. Make sure the inner tents are kept away from the outer canvas – really top-quality tents have an eyeleted waistband on the outer wall of the tent to keep it pegged out and pulled away from the inner tent. Always make sure that clips – those on the inner tents and those used for hanging larders, tent tidies and so on – face inwards not outwards and ensure, before retiring for the night, that chairs and tables are not leaning against the canvas.

Incidentally, some campers like to put a piece of heavy-duty plastic sheeting down between the ground and the inner tents to give additional warmth. Your trial weekend will show you whether you might want to adopt this practice.

Having bought the basics and tried them out, go back to buy what else is needed. You will see now why you should not start to look at camping equipment later than spring, for then you can have a trial run either over the spring bank holiday or during June and still be well equipped with exactly what you need by the time the holiday proper comes around in July or August.

What to buy
The basic camping equipment that a family of four will need is listed below and is followed by discussion of the items individually.

Tent, including groundsheet	Lighting and heating
Cooker and cooker stand	Crockery and cutlery
Beds and sleeping bags	Water containers and cool boxes
Tables and chairs	Accessories

THE TENT
The tent, the biggest and most expensive item, has to be bought carefully, and quality is the main consideration. A good-quality tent, if taken care of, should last about ten years, although in fact families tend to change them every five years or so, either because the children are growing up and no longer holiday with the family or simply because they want a more luxurious model. Incidentally, it is worth noting that tents from a reputable manufacturer, like good cars, hold their value and fetch a good price when sold second-hand or given in part-exchange.

The first point to bear in mind when buying a tent is that it must be large enough for your needs. This may seem an obvious statement, but remember that an empty tent in a showroom seems much larger than when the entire family, plus equipment, have to squeeze inside to shelter from bad weather. Living space is therefore just as important as bedroom space. Tents are sold by person or, as it is called, berth size, and it is important to buy a size larger than you think you need. A family of five, for example, should have a six-berth tent.

Families generally buy a frame tent, which consists of a canvas outer tent over a metal frame, with inner tents, or bedrooms, suspended from the frame and pegged out inside the main canvas. Ridge tents, however, are still very popular, both with backpackers and couples who do not want the bother of putting up a frame tent.

Trailer tents are becomingly increasingly popular, if the amount of space devoted to them in catalogues is anything to go by. The chief advantages of this kind of tent, which folds down neatly into its own trailer towed behind the car, are that it gives off-the-ground camping, it can be put up fairly quickly and, because much of the equipment is stowed in the trailer, space is freed in the boot of the car. Moreover, trailer tents, unlike caravans, can be stowed up-ended in the garage. In price starting at around £700 and going up to almost £2,000, trailer tents are considerably cheaper than caravans but are significantly more expensive than ordinary tents. Their cost, plus the fact that taking them over to the continent bumps up the Channel fare and towing them puts up petrol consumption, are the factors that count against them.

However, this book is concerned with the average family camper who is probably more interested in buying a frame tent than either a trailer tent or a caravan. There are about two dozen tent manufacturers selling in the United Kingdom, with French, Dutch, German and Scandinavian companies taking about two-thirds of the British market. There are over two hundred tents from which to choose, and some manufacturers offer up to a dozen models, so broad guidelines are more important than individual comparisons. The monthly magazine *Practical Camper*, under the heading 'What tent?', provides a list of manufacturers, models, floor areas, weights and recommended retail prices of new tents, which makes good comparative reading. Further details can be obtained by writing to individual manufacturers for brochures and the addresses of stockists in your area. Get manufacturers' addresses from the advertisements in the camping magazines.

When choosing a tent, consider first the frame. This is usually made of steel or light alloy tubes, but whether one type is better than the other depends on the manufacturer. A reputable tent maker will use the metal best suited to the weight of the tent, and some manufacturers offer a choice of frame. Aluminium frames are lighter and easier to handle than steel ones but tend to push up the total cost of the tent. Always take advice, for a manufacturer cutting corners will use thin tubing of a diameter too small to support the weight of the canvas, and in a large tent perhaps use only six uprights where nine would have been better: this is one of the many reasons why it is important to see a tent up if possible before buying. If the frame looks good, straight and set square and the canvas sits properly on it, the tent is a good one. It is possible to see frames actually bending when very thin metal has been used. A good tent will have extra support – generally metal triangles – on the frame where the uprights meet the horizontals. Nowadays many tents are spring-linked at the frame joints, which makes assembly a great deal easier, but on an older tent the non-spring-linked joints can be colour-coded to make putting up the tent a speedier process. Some frames have push-button adjustments which simplify pitching on uneven ground and allow for the stretching and contraction of canvas.

It is also worth asking advice on the canvas of the outer tent and the material of the inner tents. Most of us would not know what to look for if we were told that ideally the canvas of the roof, generally a heavier grade than that of the walls, should have about 240 g (8-9 oz) weight of cotton per square metre, but we would understand if we were told to look for a close-textured canvas with fine and even weaving in the cloth. Just looking can tell you a great deal. Does the outer tent sit smoothly on the frame? Are the corners squared up with the corners of the frame? Are there any bulges where zips have not been sewn in correctly or where poor stitching has caused the material to sag? Do the seams lie straight along the frame? Are load-bearing seams double stitched? In a good tent the canvas will be uniform, but in some cheap tents, manufacturers use various weights in the walls. With cheap tents the walls slope too much, which makes standing upright difficult except in the centre of the tent.

Check what the roof is made of too: in England it is important to have cotton canvas. A number of continental tents have PVC roofs, which is fine for camping in the Mediterranean where the tent is often up for the entire summer and a roof of all cotton would not be able to stand up to the continuous sunshine and the salt in the air. However, in this country, where the climate is much damper, a PVC roof can cause heavy condensation inside the tent.

Ideally the walls of the inner tents should be made of 100-percent cotton, although many manufacturers use a mixture of cotton and other materials. If totally man-made material is used, say a blend of nylon and acetate, there will be condensation problems at night. Moreover, some synthetic materials can ladder, just like a pair of tights. In a well-made inner tent the sewn-in groundsheets will be good and substantial, generally heavy-duty PVC.

Mud walling is one feature of a tent which is often the subject of furious debate: some campers are convinced that it should be on the outside of the tent; others equally certain that it should be on the inside. In case you do not know exactly what this passion-rousing mud walling is, it is that strip of PVC or similar material, about 30 cm (1 ft) or so wide, that runs along the bottom of the tent and acts like the damp-proof course in a house, preventing rain and mud from soaking into the tent. I have no strong views on mud walls, but offer this comment by Stuart Burgess, whose company, Camping Europa, makes and repairs tents. He observed that many more tents with mud walls on the outside come in for repair than those with the walling on the inside. As it can cost between £30 and £50 to mend a mud wall, it is worth giving the matter some thought. However, a greater number of tents have mud walls on the outside than on the inside, which might account for the higher number of repairs. It is also easier to damage outside mud walling by incorrect pegging out. Too often the wall is pegged down too tightly with the result that when, after a shower of rain, the canvas shrinks a little, the mud walling tears. Unpegging is always another source of damage, so use either a special tool or the hook end of a skewer peg for getting the pegs out: pulling on the mud wall to release the pegs can eventually be another cause of tears.

Damage to outside mud walls, then, is generally due to mistreatment rather than to the type of material used in the walling, or to the fact that it is on the outside. If you elect for a tent with mud walling on the inside, make sure to get a groundsheet big enough to cover the end part of the walling or you will get draughts blowing through.

Ventilation is important in a tent, particularly if the family plans to camp in a country with a warm climate. Inner tents should have mesh panels in the sides or air vents in the roofs: sometimes both are provided. The arrangement of doors, windows and canopies in the main tent should be such that a through draught is possible. Good-quality tents will have two sliders on the zip of the tent door and on the 'back' door if there is one. This means that just the top half of the door can be open, stable-fashion, to allow for ventilation. Beware of the ultra-large 'picture' windows for hot countries as these can help to make the tent a heat trap, and too much sun could cause these very big windows to distort. Check that windows are double sewn into the tent: poor seams will lead to leaks.

While on the subject of windows, check to see how the storm flaps outside the mesh windows are fastened. Tent manufacturers with an eye to important detail will use zips which keep draughts out and prevent the flaps from blowing about in a breeze. A further point about storm flaps: always roll these inwards when more ventilation is needed, so that if it rains no water will get trapped in the roll. A good tent will have detachable curtains for washing; in a cheap tent curtains are often sewn in, which means that when laundry time comes they have to be cut out.

One tent innovation that has been particularly welcome is the straight-sided kitchen area. Before its introduction it was quite easy to melt a window or burn the curtains when the stove was near a sloping window wall. These kitchen areas are particularly good for family camping, because as well as making life easier for the cook they also leave the main living part of the tent free for the rest of the family – especially useful when the weather is bad and everyone has to be inside. Some of the bigger tents have a back door near the cooking area which is useful for ventilation, particularly when meals have to be prepared on hot days. If the family is anticipating camping in the hot sun, look for a tent that has either a good deep canopy at the front (sometimes a broad shade is more welcome than the sun), or sides that can be unzipped and, by using specially provided poles, opened out to make canopies. If you cannot afford such a tent now, buy as good a one as the budget will stand and then have a canopy added later: such a job is routine to a tent repairer. Do not overdo the 'bolt-on' equipment, however, as some site proprietors charge for an additional pitch if a tent takes up too much space.

On chilly days warmth is of prime importance. A roof lining is more than just a nice way of covering up the skeleton of the frame: it also acts as insulation. This lining is supplied with a good tent but often has to be bought as an extra with a budget tent. If you are buying a tent without a roof lining – and while adding a little more comfort they are not essential – pay attention to the colour of the roof. If it is too dark, food will look gloomy, even on the brightest days. Beware of single-colour dark tents, they are very depressing to live in. Very brightly coloured tents are no longer fashionable, which is as well because certain National Parks in this country frown on gaudy tents. If you particularly want a blue tent go for a reputable manufacturer; blue is apparently a tricky dye where canvas is concerned. The current colour trend has been towards soft greens, beiges and browns.

There has been a tendency over the past few years for some manufacturers to break away from the traditional rectangular tent shape. A number have produced hexagonal models, the most revolutionary being the Mushroom made by an English company. Now a few years old, the Mushroom tent is more interesting for its frame than its shape. The aluminium alloy single construction frame works on a combination of the 'lazy tongs' baby buggy and umbrella principles. The manufacturers claim that it takes only three minutes to pull the frame out and put the canvas on, and a total of twelve minutes to have the tent completely up and pegged out, a good deal less time than it takes to erect a conventional six-berth frame tent. The Mushroom Classic, which sleeps four, costs around £345. Another of its plus points is that the frame, being aluminium, is light enough to be carried on the roof rack of a car. Always bear in mind the packing capacity of the car boot when buying a tent, remembering that no more than a third of this space should be allocated to the tent.

The recent introduction of the American Coleman tents brought a shape and concept entirely new to the British market. Interestingly enough, these beautifully made tents have come along just when there has been a growth in the sale of ridge tents. This type of tent has always been popular with those who enjoy mobile rather than static camping holidays, but over the past few years families who prefer to use the tent as a base for other activities rather than as a focus for the holiday have shown interest in the ridge type. The Coleman tents, which are a cross between a sophisticated ridge tent and an inner tent, are designed for the American way of camping and fit neatly into the slot between tents for the static camper and those for the backpacker. The American approach to camping differs from the European in that the Americans treat their tents like motels rather than homes. They do a great deal of touring and are keen on sport, so their tents serve either as overnight shelter for the family on the move or as a base camp for the huntsman away fishing or shooting in remote areas. Coleman tents could be said to be the flats or apartments of the camping world, while the lavish European tents are more like stately homes. Slick and neat, the Coleman tents with their lightweight aluminium frames and white roofs are just the job for the sightseeing family intent on spending only a couple of days on each site. But because they have only one big room without inner tents, they will not suit the family who prefer the relaxation of spending most of their holiday on one site. The Coleman Villa del Mar, a good compromise between a frame and a ridge tent, costs around £250 and can sleep three to four people comfortably. It takes only about fifteen minutes to put up, and with a maximum height of 2.5 m (8 ft) it is airy and spacious.

While on the subject of inner tents, give some thought to sleeping arrangements. Traditionally bedrooms are lined up next to each other along the back wall of the tent, an arrangement which is fine when the children are small because the parents are to hand if one of them should wake in the night: on their first camping trip in particular small children can take a couple of nights to settle down. However, a new development has been creeping into tent manufacture over the past few years whereby it is possible to obtain tents in which the 'master' bedroom is apart from the others, either immediately to the right of the entrance or still on the back wall but separated from the other rooms either by a corridor or a kitchen. This very sensible arrangement, which gives parents a small degree of privacy, is obviously possible only in the larger tents where there is more space for different layouts, but it is a point to bear in mind when buying.

Another vital requirement for your tent is a heavy-duty ground-sheet for the living area. These cost between £5 and £20, depending on size and quality.

A final piece of advice: always check the tent pack in case you need to 'top up', especially if it is a budget model. Generally speaking, the better the tent, the more the accessories.

TENT PEGS

There is more to tent pegs than most of us realize, with about a dozen variations on the basic skewer kind alone. Good-quality manufacturers generally supply an adequate number in their packs but you may have to add to the pegs supplied with a budget tent. However, it is as well to aim to carry between two and three sets of pegs per tent to allow for variations in the terrain – soft, marshy ground for example will need very different pegs from the kind used in hard, stony ground.

Generally metal bulldog pegs are used on the main guy ropes. These come in eight different lengths, starting at 9 cm (3½ in) and going up to 38 cm (15 in), with prices beginning at about 20p each. 'Soft' plastic pegs, which grip well, are becoming increasingly popular for the pegging out of the big rubber bands along the sides and at the corners of the tent. At their best in soft grassy ground, these cost about £1 for a packet of ten. Somewhat more expensive are Hitech pegs. Made by NR Components, who produce the Igloo pneumatic tent, these are 20 cm (8 in) long, are made of reinforced nylon and have a wide, toothed face for extra grip. A packet of four costs around £1.20. Skewer pegs, usually just under £1 for a packet of twelve, are used for mud walling and for pegging out the inner tents. For normal conditions twisted skewers give a good grip, but for hard or shallow ground straight skewers, sometimes used with anchor plates, are better. Wooden pegs are best for sandy soil.

Most camping shops have a display of pegs and other accessories and should be able to give advice on what is best for a particular tent. The mail-order catalogues also sell pegs. Hamptons, a leading British peg manufacturer, produces a free booklet on pegs, which is available from camping shops.

A useful tool to have is a peg extractor, which costs only around 50p. It makes pulling pegs out far easier and its use does avoid the temptation to pull on the mud walling to get difficult pegs out. Do not forget to take a mallet – or two, to speed up the pegging-out process – and a supply of spare guy ropes and tent rubbers.

BEDDING

First, sleeping bags. These can cost from under £10 to well over £70 each. From the warmth point of view, do not buy sleeping bags (particularly for use in this country) with a filling weighing less than 1077 g (38 oz). From the comfort aspect, go for bags that have a cotton rather than nylon lining. The colour or pattern of the outside of the bag is not too important, although you may find it helpful to 'colour code' bags for small children to avoid arguments about who owns the bag the orange juice has been spilt on or the chewing gum stuck to. As with duvets, feather or down sleeping bags are beautifully warm and light, but not really practical for children; machine-washable ones are preferable. Man-made fillings can be of Terylene, polyester or Holofil. Expect to pay between £10 and £15 each for a sleeping bag of reasonably good quality.

Some people like to use sleeping bag liners. These can either be made from old cotton sheets or bought from camping shops. Nylon liners, being non-porous, are not a good idea for hot countries: cotton ones are better.

What the sleeping bag rests on, either a campbed or an airbed, is very much a matter of choice. By now everyone must know that two single sleeping bags can be zipped together to make a double – providing they are both the same make and the zips match – but perhaps it is not so well known that two single airbeds, either strapped together or specially made to link together, can be more comfortable than a double airbed. Each bed can be inflated just as much as its user wishes – for example a heavy man will need a firmer bed than a slim woman. Moreover, it is cheaper to replace a single punctured airbed than a double one. Singles cost about £15, doubles about £25.

An important advantage of airbeds over campbeds is that they are kinder to the floors of inner tents. When comfort is the main consideration, rubberized cotton is the best choice of material for an airbed because it is not slippery and can 'breathe'. Some airbeds have built-in pillows, others do not, so remember to check this point.

If you prefer separate pillows you can either buy inflatable ones, which use up very little storage space, or take the familiar ones from home, which are often more comfortable but very space-consuming in the car.

Airbeds should not be inflated by mouth for, apart from this being a totally exhausting procedure, the moisture in breath will in time perish the rubber. Use a foot pump (from around £4) or, if you are really lazy, a Super Breether. This inflator/deflator, which costs about £11, works off a 12-volt car battery and can also be used to pump up rubber dinghies. Most people tend to over-inflate airbeds, which makes them very uncomfortable to sleep on. Inflate the bed to only about two-thirds of what you think necessary. Discourage children from running across airbeds, and of course never let them be used as rafts on the sea. Apart from being a highly dangerous practice, this shortens the life of an airbed as the sea water will eventually rot the fabric.

A new mattress on the market, midway between the backpacker's carry mat and a conventional airbed, is the Calipak self-inflating mattress. Similar to an airbed that works in reverse order, the Calipak comes rolled tightly and slowly inflates as the stopper is removed and air rushes in to plump out the polyurethane foam. The need for manual inflation and deflation is thus removed. To re-pack the Calipak, simply remove the stopper and squeeze out all the air by rolling the mat up again. The mattress, with a gingham-effect PVC cover, is probably best for small adults or children. It has no built-in pillow and costs £12.95, including postage and packing (by mail order only).

If you elect for campbeds, and many people feel safer off the ground, cut out draughts by putting either a blanket or a lightweight carry mat under the sleeping bag. Campbeds cost less than airbeds – expect to pay between £8 and £12 for one.

FUEL

There are three main types of fuel used for camp cooking in Europe: gas, petrol and paraffin, with gas far and away the most popular. Interestingly enough, in America, where petrol is most common, gas is regarded with mistrust. Some people still use paraffin in England, but they are generally dedicated campers and rarely families.

The two kinds of gas generally available in England are butane and propane, both of which come under the heading of liquified petroleum gas, commonly known as LPG. Butane can be used on both high- and low-pressure stoves but has the disadvantage that at low temperatures, below 6°C (42°F), it will not varporize sufficiently to burn. Propane can vaporize at well below zero and so is useful for winter campers and caravanners. However, butane, widely available in Europe, is the most popular fuel with family campers and is the gas generally offered by the rent-a-tent companies. Butane containers are generally blue, propane ones red.

There are three types of butane gas container, all pressurized. First there are the small, disposable, pierceable cartridges which have to be kept on the appliance until they are used up. These, generally used for picnic stoves and lanterns, are made by a number of manufacturers such as Camping Gaz (the biggest), Primus, EPIgas and Tilley.

Next come the disposable self-sealing cartridges which can be taken off the appliance without the gas escaping, even if it has not all been used up. These cartridges, which have been used for blow-lamps and other DIY tools for years, have traditionally been sold in hardware shops but are now available from camping shops as well. Made by Calor, Primus, EPIgas, Taymar and others, these self-sealing units are also available on the continent, but may be difficult to obtain in remote areas, so take a good supply with you to be on the safe side. (The Primus cartridge containing 454 g (16 oz) of fuel is estimated by the manufacturer to last between five and six hours on either a stove or lantern.) The advantage of self-sealing cartridges is that they can be swapped from appliance to appliance without danger. Bigger than ordinary cartridges, they may be used for stoves, lanterns and for small gas heaters. Many cartridges and self-sealing units are interchangeable, so that a lantern or stove made by one manufacturer can accept a cartridge made by another. The rapidly growing EPIgas company is one firm which makes allowances for this and, if the right adaptor is fitted, most of its products can use any gas source. The company has also produced a cylinder connecting tap which allows appliances that normally work from large containers to run off self-sealing cartridges.

Always read the instructions before fitting a gas cartridge to an appliance, and whenever possible do the job in the open air as a small amount of gas can escape as the cartridge is being attached. Never fit a cartridge in a closed tent, or near a cooker that is in use, and certainly never near anyone who is smoking. Always put discarded cartridges into dustbins as far away from the tent as possible.

If you plan to take a supply of cartridges in the boot of the car, make sure they are carefully wrapped up and that they cannot come into contact with anything sharp that could puncture them. If a lantern or picnic stove has to be packed with a partially used cartridge attached, take care to put it in an upright position and make sure that it will not tip over during the journey. It is worth keeping the boxes in which you buy lanterns and picnic stoves as these are excellent for transporting the appliances safely.

The third type of butane gas container is a refillable cylinder, available in three sizes, the 901, 454 g (1 lb), the 904 1.81 kg (4 lb) and the 907, 2.72 kg (6 lb). Camping Gaz is the main producer of these containers, which are used for stoves, some powerful single-burner cookers, gas-fired barbecues, gas heaters and some lanterns.

As to price, the smallest pressurized cartridges start at about 40p for around 40 g (1.5 oz) of butane; a 454 g (16 oz) self-sealing cartridge costs around £1.85; while the big 2.72 kg (6 lb) containers cost almost £22 initially and around £4 for refills. However, if you are a tent camper, as opposed to a caravanner, there should be no need to use the largest containers as Camping Gaz, the main supplier, sells in practically every country in Europe, so you should have no difficulty in obtaining refills if you use the middle size. Do keep the brass screw tops that come with these containers in a safe place as they can be difficult to replace.

PICNIC STOVES

Even with a camp cooker it is well worth taking a picnic stove along as well. The chances are that the cooker will be deep inside the car boot when the vacuum flask is empty and hot drinks all round are needed. There are a number of well made stoves on the market, selling for between £10 and £15. Reliable makes are Camping Gaz, Primus, Tilley and EPIgas. Some have automatic piezo ignition, useful when matches are not to hand; others have wind shields, invaluable on a breezy day. Petrol stoves come into their own when it is windy. A very sturdy petrol stove, which I have seen dropped and kicked around to demonstrate its safeness and non-leaking properties, is the Coleman Backpacker. At around £18 it costs more than the conventional picnic stove but is very well made and has a good strong flame. It runs best on special lead-free fuel costing about £1 per half litre (17 fl oz). This fuel, made by Coleman and one or two other manufacturers, is generally available from camping shops, but certainly has not the universal distribution of butane gas. If you cannot get hold of any of the lead-free fuel you can use two star petrol for the picnic stoves or lanterns for a period of up to two weeks.

A good 'halfway house' between a picnic stove and a fully fledged cooker is a two-burner stove such as the Primus 222 which packs up very neatly like a little suitcase. This stove, which costs around £30, uses separate self-sealing cartridges for each of its burners and is ideal for a couple of adults camping alone who do not need to cook family meals.

Incidentally, it is probably worth explaining that today a Primus stove, usually with a smart orange and yellow finish and running off gas, shares only its name with the famous Primus stove of years ago. The manufacturer, Primus-Sievert, now makes a range of stoves, lanterns, cookers and a recently introduced gas grill for barbecues, all of which are available from good camping shops. The old-fashioned brass Primus stove, which has to be primed with methylated spirits, has been discontinued by this company but is still made by Optimus.

CAMP COOKERS

Before buying a cooker it is as well to consider the kitchen unit that will house it. Some stands have wind shields at the sides and back, and if so you will not want these duplicated on the cooker.

Most cookers these days are low-pressure units, which means that the gas has to pass through a pressure regulator before it reaches the burners of the cooker. High-pressure stoves get their fuel directly from the gas container. The drawback to these high-pressure cookers, which are gradually being phased out, is that there is the risk of flare-ups if drops of liquid gas reach the burner and the danger of gas escaping from the cylinder if the hose is punctured. When low-pressure regulators are used, gas leaks are tiny if the tube splits or comes off the cooker. Regulators, which cost about £5, also keep the supply of gas to the burners at an even level.

Most British camping families buy cookers with two burners and a grill. In my experience, however, grills are not much good except for making toast: I have certainly never found them powerful enough for grilling either steaks or sardines, for example.

Expect to pay between £20 and £60 for a stove. Points to look out for are surfaces that are easy to clean, gentle curves rather than sharp angles, and the type of finish – stainless steel is tougher, but more expensive, than enamel, which can chip easily. The Camping Gaz Savannah double-burner stove at around £28 is simple, has no grill, no wind shield and is ideal for a camp kitchen unit. The Primus Sport, also without a grill, is beautifully finished with a stainless-steel cooking top and two brass burners, one large and one small and each with a fixed-simmer setting: it is a stove for a Cordon Bleu cook, but not cheap at around £76. For a good-quality family stove, with two burners and a grill, the Tilley Talisman at around £45, the Lytham range starting at under £20 and the Grillogaz by Camping Gaz at about £50 are all very popular and should be generally available.

Finally, do not forget to buy gas-jet prickers for clearing blockages. A package of three costs around 15p.

BARBECUES

Barbecues are becoming increasingly popular with campers. Independent travellers can take their own while a number of rent-a-tent companies have them on site, but the demand is heavy and they often have to be booked days in advance, so those renting a tent are advised to take their own as well. Many barbecues, designed with transport in mind, pack up well, and there are both charcoal-burning and gas-fired models available today.

Dealing with the gas-fired models first, the Carena mini-barbecue by Camping Gaz is sold in a box approximately 45 × 45 × 45 cm (18 × 18 × 18 in) and runs off either a 904 or a 907 gas container. Campers who already have the Carena single-burner cooker can buy the barbecue accessory which fits this model for just under £9, otherwise the complete unit costs around £22, excluding gas. If either a 904 or 907 gas container is used on the camp cooker it can, of course, be transferred to the Carena for barbecuing.

The new Champ barbecue grill by Primus also runs off either Primus or Camping Gaz containers. The practical point with this grill is that it has a deep bowl which acts as a wind shield. The Champ costs around £54 and a roasting spit is available as an extra.

The new Tilley Rotisserie is a multi-purpose cooking unit which can spit-roast or grill while at the same time heat kettles and saucepans on top of the burner. This comes complete with its own stand, runs off Camping Gaz, packs into a 'suitcase' measuring 80 × 42 × 30 cm (31½ × 16½ × 12 in) and costs over £50.

Those who prefer traditional barbecues which burn charcoal will find an enormous variety available. They vary from the traditional cast-iron circular or oblong models called hibachis ('hibachi' is Japanese for 'fire bowl') to very lightweight and compact modern ones that fold almost as flat as a bread board. When buying a cast-iron barbecue, price is a good guide to quality. Often a lower price indicates less metal content – some can have up to 30 per cent less cast iron in them than better models. But the greatest advantage of heavier barbecues is that they are more robust and do not break as easily as the cheaper models. Whatever the shape of the hibachi, make sure the fire bowl is at least 7.5 cm (3 in) deep.

One of the major importers of barbecues, Odell, offers models from the United States, Sweden and Germany, as well as the Far East. The company will supply coloured brochures, price lists, and the address of the nearest stockist to enquirers but cannot deal with personal callers as it is a distributor to the trade and does not run a retail shop. As well as a number of traditional cast-iron barbecues and some sturdy-looking Swedish models, more suitable for a permanent position in the garden than for camping, Odell supplies a neat lightweight little barbecue, the Pop-up Grill, costing around £8, that is ideal for campers in that it folds very flat and needs no screws, nuts or bolts for assembly.

For those requiring a larger barbecue, a circular cast-iron twin portable model by Odell is recommended. It is heavier than a fold-flat version and certainly more bulky, but the heavy cast-iron bowl holds the heat well. This particular model, in which the two sides fold up and clip together for transport, is specially useful for large families whose numbers fluctuate. When the whole family is present, both grids of the barbecue, each a good 30 cm (12 in) in diameter, can be used; when numbers are down, one bowl only can be used. This barbecue, which has an ash tray, costs around £21.

For those who do not like cooking at ground level, there is a folding stainless-steel barbecue. The Barberack by Desmo stands 36 cm (14 in) high and costs about £30.

Apart from fuel, the most important accessories that barbecue users need are long tongs for turning the food over, a special grip for lifting the grill plates on and off, something with which to spread the coals out and a set of skewers for kebabs. There are special brushes for putting oil on the meat, cleaners for the grill plates and various other bits and pieces available. Fuel seems to be obtainable almost everywhere but always carry a spare pack in case of emergency. Personal experience has shown that, of all the fuels, the best results can be obtained with charcoal briquettes, but do not use too many firelighters – two or three blocks are usually enough.

Certain Mediterranean camps do not allow barbecuing. If in doubt, either wait until other people light up or ask at reception.

Mid-way between barbecuing and conventional cooking comes griddle cooking. One or two companies have brought out non-stick griddles that rest on top of the two gas jets of a camping stove and which can equally well be used on a home gas or electric cooker. The non-stick griddle by Dean Bridge, 58 cm long and 25 cm wide (23 in long and 10 in wide), is a good deal bigger than the average frying pan and apparently cooks very much more quickly than conventional methods. It is also less messy as the ribbing and slant of the griddle enable excess fat to drain away down a special channel. It is not necessary to grease the griddle before use, except perhaps in the egg indentations, and it is perfectly possible to cook bacon, eggs, chops, sausages, mushrooms and tomatoes, a good family-sized mixed grill in fact, all at once. The griddle, economical on fuel and easy to clean, costs around £14, but make sure that it fits on your camp stove. It fits best those cookers where the sides are not higher than the gas jets.

CAMP KITCHENS

Camp kitchens are beanstalk arrangements basically designed to house a cooker but which can be built up to form the most elaborate kitchen units. The shelves are generally made of nylon-coated wire mesh, although there are some solid-shelf models available. To begin with, buy just the basic unit consisting of a top shelf, usually with a wind shield and splash-back, to house the cooker and two storage shelves underneath. This should cost between £16 and £20. Look for stability rather than style. The Hago Beanstalk is sturdy and popular, SMS and Falcon also produce well-made stable units and Tilley makes a good basic table stand for a stove at about £12.

Once you have your basic unit it is a matter of choice whether extensions are added. There are special units available to take washing-up bowls, plate racks, waste bins, kitchen-paper rolls and even vanitory units complete with shaving mirror. It is very much a matter of opinion but I personally find too many specially designed units are space consuming while not always used to maximum efficiency.

COOKING UTENSILS, CROCKERY AND CUTLERY

Although it is perfectly possible to use home saucepans, crockery and cutlery for the first couple of years' camping, it is well worth buying a camping kettle with a fold-down handle immediately. These cost from about £3 and are much more convenient to pack than conventional kettles. Do not buy one with a capacity of less than 1.7 l (3 pt). For convenience keep the kettle, already filled with water, close to the picnic stove in the back of the car on the journey, and remember to keep it topped up *en route* between camp sites.

Nesting aluminium saucepans with detachable metal handles are the best for camping, but do not buy cheap ones or they will be too thin and the handle will not be secure enough. Nesting sets of saucepans cost from about £10 to £20.

If you use a pressure cooker at home, by all means take it camping. It certainly speeds up cooking and cuts down on saucepan washing-up. However, it is not advisable to try one for the first time on a camp site.

There is a big range of lightweight plastic 'crockery' to choose from, Melamine being the toughest and the most long-lasting as well as the most expensive. Do not buy made-up packs of camping crockery, but stick to the basics of just one large plate, one small plate, one bowl and one mug with a handle for each person. A large Melamine bowl for fruit or salad is a useful addition, and possibly a couple of spare mugs. If you must have glasses for wine, choose short, thick tumblers, and take an earthenware jug if you intend to make fresh coffee. There is no need to take space-consuming teapots as tea can be made in the mugs with teabags. Cutlery sets, with a knife, fork and spoon in individual cases, are fine for lone campers but not such a good idea for families as the sets never get put back in the cases. It is easiest just to get one knife, fork, large spoon and teaspoon for each member of the family. Also have a supply of general teaspoons as these seem to be in constant use and frequently get lost.

Wooden spoons are useful, both for cooking and as salad servers. Add a couple of serving spoons, a serrated bread knife and one good-quality small sharp knife, a tin opener, a corkscrew and crown cap opener. An insulated butter container is useful. Ideally all the camping equipment, including saucepans, crockery and cutlery, should be kept in one place and used only for holidays. Include chopping boards in this holiday 'pack'. You will probably need two when camping, which can double up as bread boards and serving platters for meat, cheese and cakes.

TABLES AND CHAIRS

If you already have lightweight garden chairs, these will be fine for camping as long as they are of the correct height for the table. Rather than have to replace the chairs, go for a table with adjustable legs – these are also convenient when camping on uneven ground. When choosing a table, make sure that it is well finished: if there is a rim it should be well fastened down so that it does not become a crumb trap. Card-playing families find that tables with edges can impede the odd sleight of hand sometimes needed in games of skill. Tables with clip-on extensions are recommended for families of four or more – camping tables are never very large and you do not want to be short of space for food. Expect the starting price for an average table with folding legs to be around £20. The most expensive cost around £30.

The price variation in chairs is enormous, with aluminium alloy frames and nylon covers at the lower end of the range. A plus point with aluminium, which is lighter than steel, is that it does not have to be painted, but it is soft and can scratch. Steel chairs tend to be more sturdy and seem to have better-quality seats. Canvas is more comfortable to sit on than nylon, particularly in hot climates. Chairs that fold sideways are easier to tuck under tables at meal times, but do not pack as flat as front-folding chairs. Broad armrests are more comfortable than just metal sides. Look out for chairs that are going to be simple to repair when the seat wears, and if space is at a premium take fishing stools for the children. Expect to pay around £12 for a basic steel-frame chair with a canvas seat, arms and back rest. Lafuma, Navro and Walker, stocked by reputable camping shops, are reliable makers of tables and chairs.

Useful for families starting from scratch is a table and chair set made by Plein Air that packs neatly up into a case and costs around £30 from camping shops.

LIGHTING

Gas lanterns are the most popular way of lighting tents. They can be hung from the ceiling (but not too close to the canvas) or put on the table for either indoor or outdoor meals: many campers consider it dangerous to hang gas lanterns from the ceiling of the tent because of the fire hazard. However, there is also the danger of the lantern getting knocked over when it stands on a table. So where you put it is very much a matter of personal choice. Lanterns have a soft glow, just right for camping when people are sitting quietly talking, but low-powered ones are not always suitable for reading by, so check the brightness of the light when buying. The light given off by most gas lanterns is equivalent to about an 80-watt electric bulb; lanterns in this category cost around £15 each. EPIgas make a particularly attractive light with a circular glass shade, similar in appearance to an old-fashioned oil lamp, which costs about £12. Two lanterns, the Camping Gaz Symphony, about £30 and the Primus automatic lantern, about £25 both with automatic ignition and both providing light equivalent to 100 watts, possess a clever device – a base which slides up to protect the globe when the lantern is in transit.

Petrol lamps, particularly the two-mantel variety, give off a very bright light. The beautifully made and very safe and stable Coleman Easi-lite costs around £23. The famous Tilley storm lamp, which has been popular for years, uses paraffin and, like the petrol lamps, gives off a certain amount of warmth as well as light. It costs about £27. Remember to take spare mantels for all types of lantern.

Strip lights which run off a 12-volt car battery are excellent. They give a good bright light, are very safe and can be clipped inside inner tents – useful for children who like to read in bed while their parents still need the gas lantern in the main part of the tent. Strip fluorescent lights, which come complete with cable, clips and sometimes a hook, vary in price according to wattage and length and cost from around £9 each.

It is advisable to have at least one torch with you when camping. Many children feel more secure if they can have a torch near them at night, and of course a torch is also useful too for night trips to the loo. For general family camping the big rubber torches like truncheons are a good investment. They can stand a certain amount of mis-use, are water-resistant and could, if necessary, double up as a weapon.

COOL BOXES, HEATERS AND WATER CARRIERS

Cooling aids range from soft, folding bags to rigid containers that take chemical-action freezer sachets, and now proper refrigerators are available that run off gas containers, or the camp site electricity supply or, in some cases, off a car battery. Most popular with campers are the rigid cool boxes, but make sure you get one deep enough to take bottles of wine and ensure that you are well enough provided with freezer sachets to have two in the box, two in the cold store and two set by for emergencies. Be prepared to be charged a small amount for having sachets frozen in France. Some camp sites refuse to accept the soft variety because when they get old they tend to split, so for safety get the rigid packs. Write the family name on the pack in ink that will not smudge when it gets wet, otherwise it will be impossible to identify which is yours among the hundred or so identical sachets in the camp freezer. On many European sites it is common for blocks of ice to be sold twice daily – some sites do not like having their freezers full of sachets.

Cool boxes start at about £7 for a 20-l (34 pt) and go up to £20 or so for a 38-l (64 pt) capacity model. Some have all-in-one shopping-basket-type handles; others have separate handles, one on either side. The latter is easier for two people to carry when it is full and heavy as each has his or her own handle. The lid of the box should fit snugly and firmly and the outer and inner walls should be strong enough to stand the occasional bump or knock.

Heaters can be useful, even on the continent, for chilly evenings. There are two kinds of gas heater on the market. The majority are reflector-bowl heaters with prices starting at around £27 for a 1.5-kilowatt model, running off a 904 1.81 kg (4 lb) gas container. However, the fairly new catalytic chemical heaters are probably safer. They too run off gas but burn without a flame and will never catch fire. They are efficient and quite expensive – an EPIgas model costs about £37.

Water carriers do not have to be enormous. There are cold water taps on all sites and it is often possible to fill carriers at village pumps *en route* for the camp. The 10 l (2 gal) size, costing about £2, is probably the easiest for children to manage. Also you can if you wish take a roll-up water carrier with a tap as an extra and hang it up in the tent – this makes filling kettles easier. Complete with hanger, it also costs about £2.

ACCESSORIES

Some camping accessories can be classed as luxuries; others are essential. From the practical point of view, the most essential accessory is a washing-up bowl, followed by all that goes with it – detergent, dish cloth, drying-up towels and rubber gloves. A rectangular bowl packs better than a round one. A lidded bucket for soaking dirty clothes in and for carrying them to and from the washing and drying area is another necessity, as are clothes pegs, a line and some soap powder. A fold-up plastic-covered metal clothes airer for damp towels is very useful both for outside the tent in the daytime and inside at night. Some camp sites do not allow washing lines near the tents but find these airers acceptable. Take disposable plastic bags for rubbish and wire tags with which to close them before dumping them in the camp dustbin.

The final essential pieces of cleaning equipment are a dustpan and soft brush for the inside of the tent and a stiff brush for cleaning the groundsheet and the under side of inner tents and for giving the canvas of the outer tent a brush down before packing up. Once again, try to keep all these items for camping only: it makes packing simpler and avoids having to denude the house each time you go away.

To keep track of all those small items that are always going missing, such as sun tan oil, hair brushes, sun glasses and so on, a hanging canvas tent tidy with about sixteen pockets of various sizes is essential: these cost around £6.

If there is no larder space in the camp kitchen, a free-standing version with mesh sides is useful for food that need not or cannot be stored in the cool box. A wardrobe rail, if it is not supplied with the tent, to hang between the two main bedrooms avoids the necessity of clothes spending all their time creased in a case. Remember to take some coat hangers. Hanging hooks that attach to the tent frame are useful because they do not take up much packing space; they can be used for tea towels, dry swimming gear, pyjamas and so on.

Items taking up more space than they earn come in the luxury class. Children tend to want to take elaborate toys, games and gigantic books, but try to keep them to card games and paperbacks, a badminton set and some balls for beach games.

Families with very small children might find it necessary to take a portable toilet. These can be very elaborate and expensive, but two moderately-priced and simple ones are the Racasan Cruiser S which is small and sturdy, and the Elsan mini-toilet which weighs only 1.81 kg (4 lb): both cost around £16 each.

Nowadays most good European sites have English-style lavatories, but very young children can still be scared of using them to begin with. It is always worth taking a home pottie, a known and familiar object, on a child's first camping trip. Even though the child may have outgrown it at home, it may be useful for the first couple of days.

A folding cot may be an essential item rather than a luxury when you are taking a baby camping. Complete with mattress, a canvas cot on a folding aluminium frame costs about £23, or from around £14 without a mattress.

Mirrors are essential, and easily forgotten when assembling your equipment. There are special ones for camping that clip on to the frame of the tent.

That is it as far as buying the basic camping equipment is concerned. There are many other things you can take along, but they will be dealt with in subsequent chapters.

Addresses

Caseys Camping Ltd,
Brunel Way,
Ashton Gate,
Bristol BS3 2JB.

Customers in Northern Ireland should send their orders to:
Caseys Camping Ltd,
Rear of Halfords,
Bow House,
Bow Street,
Lisburn,
Co Antrim.

Customers in Eire should send their orders to:
Caseys Camping Ltd,
Camping & Sport of Celbridge,
Industrial Estate,
Celbridge,
Co Kildare.

Scout Shops Ltd,
Churchill Industrial Estate,
Lancing,
West Sussex BN15 8UG.
The brochure gives the names and addresses of the 15 camping and outdoor centres run by Scout Shops.

Blacks Camping and Leisure,
10/11 Catford Broadway,
London SE6 4SP.

Coleman UK Inc,
Unit 2,
Parish Wharf Estate,
Harbour Road,
Portishead,
Bristol BS20 9DA.

Coleman sells through a number of camping shops, including Scout
Shops, Caseys, Blacks and the Co-op. There is a display room in
Bristol where customers can view. Write for catalogue and name
and address of nearest stockist.

Camping Europa Ltd,
247 School Road,
Birmingham 14.

The Mushroom Tent Company,
Broxmore House,
Cliftonville Road,
Dorking,
Surrey RH4 2BR.

For booklets on camping accessories and tent pegs write to:
The Hampton Works (Stampings) Ltd,
Twyning Road,
Stirchley,
Birmingham B30 2XZ.

Super Breether. This British-made accessory should be stocked by
most camping shops but write to the distributors for the address of
your nearest stockist if you cannot find it.

I & M Steiner Ltd,
Reynard Mills Trading Estate,
Windmill Road,
Brentford,
Middlesex TW8 9LY.

Elsan Ltd,
Richborough Works,
Sandwich,
Kent.

The Calipak self-inflating mattress is mail order only and is made
by:
Caligen Foam Ltd,
Broad Oak,
Accrington,
Lancs BB5 2BS.

Although Camping Gaz products are stocked by most camping shops, not all have the complete range. The company produces a broadsheet giving the full product range as well as a list of the European countries where its gas cartridges and containers are available. There is also information on the sheet on repairs and servicing.

Camping Gaz (GB) Ltd,
126-130 St Leonards Road,
Windsor,
Berks.

Primus stoves, lanterns and cookers are made by:
Primus-Sievert UK Ltd,
PO Box No 562,
9/11 Gleneldon Road,
Streatham,
London SW16 2AU.

Write to Primus for their Leisure Line brochure and nearest stockist.

EPIgas,
NR Components,
Lydgate,
Todmorden,
Lancs OL14 7DR.

A range of paraffin and petrol cookers which have to be primed, as well as meths stoves which do not, are made by:
A B Optimus Ltd,
Sanders Lodge Estate,
Rushden,
Northants NN10 9BQ.

Although Tilley says its products are stocked by good hardware shops, department stores and camping outlets, it can be quite hard running them down. The products are well made and reliable, so it is worth sending off for the illustrated brochure and name of nearest stockist.

The Tilley Lamp Co Ltd,
Dunmurry,
Belfast BT17 9JA.

Lytham Leisure Products,
Preston Road,
Lytham,
Lancs.

SMS,
Sheet Metal Shapes,
105 Carpenters Road,
London E15 2DU.

Hago Products Ltd,
Shripney Road,
Bognor Regis,
West Sussex PO22 9NH.

Falcon Works,
Hanworth Road,
Sunbury on Thames,
Middlesex.

Racasan Odex Ltd,
Ellesmere Port,
South Wirral.

Desmo Ltd,
Pensnett,
Brierley Hill,
West Midlands DY6 7NR.

Frank Odell Ltd,
70 High Street,
Teddington,
Middlesex.

Dean Bridge (Manufacturing) Ltd.,
Rofton Works,
Hooton,
South Wirral L66 7NG.

Lafuma and Narva tables and chairs are distributed by:
NR Components Ltd,
Lydgate,
Todmorton,
Lancs OL14 7DR.

Walker tables and chairs are distributed by:
L. Freeman & Sons Ltd,
1 Bigg Market,
Newcastle upon Tyne NE1 1UP.

2
Rented Tents and Hired Packs

A great many people now totally committed to camping started off by renting a fully furnished tent already on site or hiring a camping pack containing all the necessary equipment, including the tent. Some enjoy renting so much that they stay loyally with the same company year after year. Others rent for a couple of years until, fired by the thought of the freedom it gives, they buy their own gear and strike off on their own. But new recruits to renting keep coming along, because as well as the first-timers there are also the families who feel that they have served their time loading the car and putting up frame tents and who now just want to relax in agreeable surroundings.

The rent-a-tent market has grown steadily since it began in the sixties and is now so well established, mainly in France, but increasingly in Germany, Switzerland, Austria, Spain and Italy, that the big holiday organizations are taking an interest as well. Now, a number of big tour operators such as Thomson Holidays with their subsidiary Portland Camping, Ellerman Travel and others are entering this field. So it seems likely that the rent-a-tent market is here to stay.

Rented tents: the background

Rent-a-tent holidays began when pioneers Margaret and Jim Cuthbert started Canvas Holidays. In common with most families with children – the Cuthberts have four – Margaret and Jim could only get their ration of sun by camping abroad. It was while wrestling with his own equipment that Jim Cuthbert was suddenly struck by the idea that even more families might be tempted to go camping if they could be spared the effort of dragging all the gear across the Channel. So Canvas Holidays started in 1966 and almost twenty years later is still very much the market leader, able in 1982 to offer tent accommodation on over ninety sites in five European countries.

Ten years after Canvas started there were still only a dozen rent-a-tent companies in existence. By the late seventies however, there were well over sixty and officially over one hundred by 1982, though the true figure was probably nearer two hundred if all the small companies offering just a couple of tents on one site, and not advertising nationally, were taken into consideration. The boom began in the mid-seventies, by which time the word had begun to get around – rent-a-tent companies rely heavily on word of mouth recommendation – that this type of holiday was enjoyable as well as value for money. A couple of good summers, plus rising inflation, helped the market even further, so by the end of the decade the good companies had become well established and new operators had entered the field.

However, in 1982 some concerns went to the wall and it was not just the recession that accounted for their failure.

Apart from not fully appreciating the complexity of the booking system, some of the new companies regarded the idea as a business venture rather than a service and did not grasp that actual camping experience is as valuable as capital in this kind of enterprise. A proprietor or manager of a rent-a-tent company who is also an experienced camper will be able to tell whether it is worth taking pitches on certain sites: he or she will know the pitfalls and the hidden snags. Someone without any experience of camping can be fobbed off by wily camp site owners with inferior pitches and will not know, until the clients start complaining, that they have chosen some that are too much in the shade, too much in the sun, too close to the toilet block, too close to the disco, and so on.

At least companies coming into the business today do not have the problems that Canvas faced in the early days when suspicious French camp-site proprietors did not immediately grasp the principle of rented tents. They just did not believe it when told that a certain number of tents would be pitched on their site for the summer and that they, the proprietors, would be paid for the pitch whether the tent was occupied or not. Many thought that the devious British were up to some strange dealings; they agreed to the arrangement, but reluctantly. Attitudes have changed wonderfully over the past nineteen years, though, and site owners are now only too delighted to accept the financial security that the British companies bring. Indeed, the business of getting good pitches on the best sites has become very cut-throat over the past few years, and most rent-a-tent companies have nasty stories to tell of prices being upped and pitch numbers changed. Not all the bad behaviour is on the side of the French site proprietors, either.

In general, however, a good deal of benefit has come out of the presence of the rent-a-tent companies. Because of their buying power, companies have been able to persuade site owners to put in or speed up the installation of new facilities that otherwise might have been delayed or never provided at all. Both Canvas and Eurocamp say they have seen swimming pools and tennis courts appear, toilet blocks extended and improved, and shops smartened up. A wider range of goods has appeared in some camp shops and prices have often come down to a realistic level. Even a comparative newcomer, Inn-Tent, part of the Wallace-Arnold concern, which started in 1980, was able to put pressure on a site to install a brand-new swimming pool where none had existed previously. The company, whose policy is to find small high-quality sites, many of them inland, had come across an excellent camp in the Charente region of France but felt that as an inland site it would not attract families unless it had a pool. Once he knew that a certain number of pitches was guaranteed, the site owner had a pool installed and ready for use for the 1981 season.

For of course the site owner cannot lose. If the tents remain unoccupied during the season, it is the rent-a-tent company that bears the loss of revenue, not the camp. So the days of having to explain to a doubtful owner what rented tents are all about are long over. But other problems have arisen. Today new companies are hard pressed to find good sites with pitches to spare, and many of the best coastal sites have been creamed off years ago by the well-established concerns. There is a danger, when a camp-site owner is too anxious to rent out pitches, that a particular site can turn into a little England with rows and rows of tents all filled with British campers: in 1981, for example, one particular site in the western Mediterranean had eight British companies on it. Not everyone going abroad wants to be surrounded by their fellow countrymen! In such a situation the choice for the new companies is either to go for lower-grade sites or, if they are interested and energetic enough and keen to provide the best for their clients, to look for new, high-quality sites. For the camping scene is not static and new sites are being opened all the time, even in the crowded seaside resorts, although not as quickly as some would like.

Once the pitches have been negotiated, the tents and furnishings have to be bought – Canvas reckons that today it costs around £1,250 to buy and furnish a top-quality, fully equipped tent – an exercise which brings its own crop of difficulties. A number of new and inexperienced companies run into trouble getting their equipment through French customs and on to the site. The paperwork is prolific and the traps for the unwary endless, but it is useless taking a short cut, for unless a rent-a-tent company abides by the rules it can find itself in difficulty with the authorities and faces the possibility of having its gear impounded.

Even when the equipment has been safely delivered and the tents are up and furnished, the problems do not stop. Tents, unlike hotels or apartment blocks which tend to stay put when they are up, can move once they are pitched (if only a small amount). They need constant supervision and often have to be re-pegged between one family moving out and another coming in. The contents have to be checked and some items replaced, gas containers have to be replenished and, if the worst happens and a storm wreaks havoc, complete tents have to be replaced. This is where the companies with stores in France can score. Even though couriers have spares, their supplies are limited. In an emergency it is far quicker to rush fresh stock from a French depot than to have to go through all the complications of getting it across the Channel. Emergencies are by their nature sudden, so by the time the replacements have arrived from England the crisis may have passed, but the holidaymaker, having to make do with temporary equipment, may not be too happy.

It is fair to say, however, that major disasters such as the tent blowing down are rare rather than everyday occurrences. But the infrastructure of a rent-a-tent company is important. It is invisible to the customer most of the time but it is one of the factors that helps to keep the company in business and enables it to weather the ups and downs which cause less well-established companies to fail.

It is probably worth pointing out here that when under half a dozen companies fail out of a hundred or so that continue in the rent-a-tent business, the risk to the holidaymaker is not great. However, it is important for customers to know that the holiday they book in the winter and finish paying for in June will still be available in July or August. Because most of the independent rent-a-tent companies work on a direct-sell basis and are therefore not members of ABTA (the Association of British Travel Agents), this assurance is even more important. From the point of view of those taking conventional package holidays put together by the big tour operators, the advantage of ABTA is that it underwrites its members, so that if a tour operator or travel agency fails ABTA will provide certain financial compensation to those who have lost their holiday. But what happens to the customers if a rent-a-tent company fails? How to avoid shaky operators will be dealt with later in this chapter, but fortunately, most of these companies, particularly the well-established ones, are self-sufficient and can bail themselves out if things go wrong.

As well as knowing that they have chosen a company that is financially sound, prospective holidaymakers need to know, particularly if they have never been camping before, what exactly it is they are buying in a rent-a-tent package. To avoid making an expensive mistake when booking, they should take time to pick a holiday that is going to please all the family. Careful comparative study and judicious reading between the lines of the different brochures should enable an informed decision to be made.

Rent-a-tent companies: choosing and booking

The rent-a-tent market caters for absolutely everyone: for families who want a seaside holiday, for people who prefer to go inland, whether for a rural or city-based holiday, for youngsters who want a lively social life with plenty of evening entertainment, for retired couples, and so on. There are camping holidays for families using their own cars, as well as coach/tent and fly/tent holidays on offer. And as with any other type of holiday, there is a wide price range, so that people from all income brackets as well as all backgrounds are catered for.

Usually when you book a package holiday you collect brochures from and have a chat with the local travel agent. As the majority of camping holidays are sold direct to the public, there is no travel agent to give advice. So talk to someone who has already been on this type of holiday – it should not be too difficult nowadays to find such a person.

Send away for brochures from four or five companies. The big companies start advertising in the national press just before Christmas and continue for the next few months. If things are not going too well they will still be advertising in May and June. Should you miss the newspaper advertisements, and France is your proposed destination, get the annual holiday guide from the French Government Tourist Office (address on page 88), which gives the names and addresses of many organizations offering tent and caravan holidays. The publication which comes out each January, is free, but send 50p for packing and postage.

Competition is keen between the big companies because they all want to get as many firm bookings as possible early in the year. All this is good from the consumer's point of view, as it ups the quality of the end product. For example, when one company introduced sprung beds with proper mattresses, others in the same league followed suit. As soon as one company brought in electric or gas refrigerators, some others felt they had to do the same, though refrigerators have not become as commonplace as 'proper' beds. Now there are non-stick saucepans, sunshades, salad servers, welcoming bottles of wine, the use of the company dinghy or barbecue on site, and all manner of extras to entice the customer to camp with one particular company rather than another. What concerns the camper more than all the embellishments, however, is the need to know that he or she has chosen a reliable company. It would be little consolation to be promised the use of a windsurfer in January only to find that there was not even a tent in July.

The first test of whether a company is for you is plain common sense. A picture showing a young couple dashing into the sea holding hands, with the banner headline 'Plenty of fun – from only £49' is not going to appeal to a family with four children under the age of twelve, just as an advertisement showing a couple of six-year-olds happily building sand castles is not going to attract a couple of single women in their early twenties. So read the advertisements carefully before sending away for the brochures. When these arrive, check how long the company has been in operation: the good firms usually give this information. If a company is fairly new, find out if it has the financial backing of a big organization. Do not be impressed by over-lavish brochures. Anyone can get a booklet printed; the quality of the glossy page has nothing to do with the quality of the tents on site. Big colour brochures are extremely expensive to produce and a careful company may well keep its brochures to a modest size, investing its money instead in better equipment.

Check whether a thumbnail sketch is given of the company and do not be too cynical about all those letters from satisfied customers. They are usually genuine and not simply culled from the questionnaires that rent-a-tent companies are so fond of sending out. Apparently a great many people dash off letters of appreciation while still on holiday. Some companies give the occupation of those who send letters of praise – quite a clever move, in that it allows prospective customers to assess the breadth of the social mix. The comments from journalists are worth reading, because they often make pertinent points of value to the prospective camper.

It is important to read the booking form in detail, and the more detail that is given the better. Check insurance: it is not automatically included, but nowadays most car-based camping companies include personal insurance as part of the package and recommend that extra insurance be taken out for the car. On the whole, the coach/tent companies seem not to include insurance in their packages.

Remember too to look at the 'nuts and bolts' of the holiday, details such as the time you may occupy your tent. It may sound trivial in January, but when you turn up hot and tired at around midday in a crowded Mediterranean resort in July only to find that the tent you booked is not available until 3.00 p.m. it can seem like a major disaster, particularly if you have a couple of querulous children in the back of the car. If you want to camp close to friends, check if this is possible, as not all companies can arrange adjacent tents. Be prepared for all eventualities; read the cancellation clauses before you book. These should be clearly given. You generally lose your deposit when you cancel and, depending on when you cancel, between 33 per cent and 90 per cent of the total cost of the holiday.

Finally, if you are still uncertain whether you have selected the right firm, and many first-time campers in particular need plenty of reassurance, telephone the company of your choice. The good organizations welcome genuine telephone queries, and some do not even mind personal callers, as their brochures say. However, if you do call in, do not be put off if all you see is a busy, humming office. Rent-a-tent companies are not travel agents: they do not set out to attract passing trade, so there are no evocative posters or tempting brochures on display. Like any other direct-sell organization they are mainly concerned with the behind-the-scenes work of getting holiday bookings processed.

SITE DESCRIPTION

When it comes to site descriptions, companies whose brochures show photographs of the actual camp rather than pretty pictures of children romping on the beach are preferable. As to the written description, once the important scene-setting piece is over you will need to know how far the beach is from the site – *exactly*, not 'just a short walk' but the actual distance. Most brochures concerned with France now give the French star rating as well as anything from eight to twelve symbols to help build up a picture of a site.

Some companies quote the actual site names in their brochures, which is quite useful as you can then cross-refer with the Michelin Guide. It always helps when the type of washing and sanitary installations, of major importance to English campers, are mentioned. You will also want to know the standard of the restaurant. Personal comments from the rent-a-tent personnel who have visited the site are important, and show that homework has been thoroughly done.

COSTS

When it comes to comparing prices, you need to keep your wits about you. To quote some examples: most companies offer fourteen-day holidays, but Inn-Tent has a basic twelve-day holiday starting any day of the week, while Canvas has extremely flexible, if somewhat complicated, Travelplans which enable campers to choose when they want to cross and allow them to stay away any length of time as long as they spend a minimum of six nights under canvas.

When costing your holiday, look out for site supplements, which can be as much as £4 per tent per day in the high season – an extra £56 on a fortnight's holiday can be quite a blow. When it is levied, this extra charge is always shown clearly in the brochure but not always in the same place as the other charges. Most companies offer reduced rates for youngsters between three and fourteen, but the policy on charging for infants varies.

Always check whether you have to pay extra for the use of gas or any other articles. Some companies offering coach/tent packages have a system whereby the coach and cross-Channel car and tent hire are included in the basic package, but for self-caterers there is usually a hire charge, between £16 and £20 a fortnight, for a cooking pack. This includes cooker, pans, crockery, cutlery, and so on, but there may be even a further charge for hiring a cool box and a gas lantern. Certain companies in this field also ask for a returnable deposit on arrival to cover the cost of any damage to the tent or equipment.

Finally, if you can travel outside peak holiday time, look for the very good low-season offers. If you have to go in July or August and cost is a consideration, find out what reductions are offered for either mid-week or night Channel crossings.

EQUIPMENT

All brochures list the gear that is included in a package and some actually show photographs of it. There are subtle differences: for example, some companies include cutlery, others do not; some have cool boxes while others use either gas or electric refrigerators; and a couple now supply sunshades, a particularly good idea on Mediterranean sites. The quality of the cooking equipment is important. Non-stick good quality saucepans, such as offered by Canvas Holidays, make life easier for the cook.

Another important item to check, if you are keen on comfort, is which firms supply sprung beds with mattresses and which still offer airbeds or campbeds. These days most companies have sprung double beds, but not all that many run to sprung single beds as well. Families with very small children should find out if a cot can be hired.

Remember that sleeping bags and pillows nearly always have to be supplied by the camper. If there are sprung beds, don't forget to take fitted sheets to cover the mattresses.

One great advantage of a fully furnished tent is that, because it is semi-permanent, the equipment on the whole is far sturdier and often more comfortable than the lightweight gear that the self-contained camper has to hump around. However, a company has yet to come up with top-quality canvas chairs to replace the plastic-seated ones most seem to use; these are good and robust, but uncomfortable to sit on in very hot weather.

As to the tent itself, some companies are offering bigger and better models each year and this can only be a plus when it means that there is more space in the inner tents to walk round the beds.

Good companies give dimensions as well as tent plans in their brochures. This may be of particular use to families for whom the arrangement of sleeping accommodation is important (see page 25).

Check also how often the tents are replaced. Reliable companies renew them every two years and some organizations have tents specially made for their own use with good heavy-duty zips and top-quality canvas. This is because, unlike private tents, which are usually put up only a couple of times a year at the most, rented tents are in constant use during the season and have to be strong enough to stand up to plenty of wear and tear and even mis-use.

Finally, try to find out the size of the pitch. Many car-based companies catering for the family market reckon that a maximum 100 sq m (120 sq yd) to 84 sq m (100 sq yd) is generally a good size; a number of coach-based companies settle for 80 sq m (95 sq yd) while some corner-cutting companies and those offering accommodation to youngsters, who do not seem to mind being packed in like sardines, might offer smaller than this. A pitch of less than 60 sq m (71 sq yd) might be somewhat cramped.

COURIERS

There are two schools of thought on couriers: some companies use single undergraduates, while others prefer married couples, but a few organizations (generally those who just offer tents as part of a general self-catering programme) do not have any couriers on site. Family campers certainly need to choose a company that uses couriers. As well as showing you to your pitch when you arrive and explaining the geography and rules of the site, the couriers can generally offer information on local activities, can replace gas cylinders when they run out, are able to lend extra chairs and supply cots, possibly organize baby sitters, and be on hand to help in emergencies. It is a matter of personal choice whether you select a company which uses young or mature couriers. There is keen competition for these jobs and successful applicants, particularly with the good companies, have thorough training before setting up on site. So, whatever the age of the courier, you can expect, with a reliable company, that he or she will be competent.

OVERNIGHT STOPS

Most companies that have sites in the Mediterranean and are offering car-based holidays have set up a network of overnight stops using either reasonably priced hotels or Mocamps tents. More about Mocamps later. If distances are worked out carefully beforehand, campers can plan their own overnight stops, either finding a hotel as they drive along or booking directly in advance with Mocamps. However, anyone wanting the security of knowing a bed is booked for the night, particularly a family with young children, will probably prefer the peace of mind that the rent-a-tent booking service gives. Companies that offer overnight stops usually provide a mileage chart, so that driving distances between ports, stops and final destination can be calculated. At least two companies, Canvas and Eurocamp, subject all bookings received to a feasibility study and, if they feel a camper has over-estimated the amount of driving they think they can cope with in one day, suggest either an earlier Channel crossing or an extra overnight stop. Think carefully when estimating driving times, for getting used to the right-hand side of the road takes a little while, and if you are driving to the Mediterranean make allowances for the fact that you will be unaccustomed to the warmer climate. It is all too easy to lose concentration on a long, hot motorway drive, particularly after an early-morning start.

TRAVEL PACKS

When they send you all the documents needed for your holiday – tickets, insurance papers, maps, car stickers and so on – some companies also provide a travel pack which consists of a wallet containing information that might be useful on your trip. This travel pack can show how well the company has thought through the whole concept of the service it offers.

Some companies, however, feel that such packs add unnecessarily to the cost of a holiday and do not offer them at all.

Do not forget to take the brochures on holiday as well as all the appropriate documents and the travel pack, if supplied, when you set off. You will then be able to check that the site description is correct. If there are any complaints, make a note there and then and write to the company as soon as you get home.

Renting a tent: who offers what

The rent-a-tent market is divided into two main categories: the larger section, consisting of companies that offer car-based tent holidays and, more and more, caravan holidays; and the rapidly expanding coach-based section, increasingly aimed at families, but also at young single people. Suntopper, for example, aimed specifically at the 18 to 30 age group offers coach-based camping holidays in the south of France. So does Sunsport, an offshoot of the well known children's activity holiday company PGL. Sunsport also has a fly/camp holiday. A growing number of organizations is providing this type of air-based holiday, for as the Mediterranean becomes more and more crowded and camp sites are sought in places such as Israel, Iceland, North Africa and even Canada, travel by car or coach becomes impracticable.

Campers travelling to the continent from Eire should be aware of the fact that a growing number of car-based companies operating from the UK are now providing direct sea travel from Rosslare to Le Havre or Cherbourg.

The services provided by the various rent-a-tent companies are listed on the following pages. Not everyone is mentioned. Apart from the half dozen or so companies who did not reply when the book was being compiled, space does not permit every company in existence to be included. Those that are mentioned have been around for some time, offer a particularly good service or, if they are new, often have the financial backing of a larger company.

CAR-BASED HOLIDAYS: TOTALLY TENT

Canvas Holidays

This, the biggest company of its kind in the country, has resisted any temptation to diversify into caravans or to link up with any other travel concern and so presents a very clear picture. Since 1966 Canvas Holidays has stuck to its very successful formula of providing high-quality tents (it has kept to the same design for the past ten years) furnished with the top grade equipment. In 1982, electric refrigerators were introduced on certain sites, and in 1983 electric light. The company offers holidays on eighty-nine seaside and inland sites in France, Spain Switzerland, Austria and Italy. Last year the company chalked up another first by providing as an additional extra, activity and special interest pursuits on certain sites in the low and mid seasons. These include cycling, walking, bird-watching, wind-surfing and riding as well as lectures on history, wine, wild-life and so on.

Ellerman Camping Holidays

This new company is an offshoot of the well established Ellerman travel concern and sells its camping holidays nationwide through travel agents as well as accepting direct bookings. There are seven car-based sites on the west coast of France and two coach-based sites on the Mediterranean, one in France and the other in Spain. Ellerman have now also taken over Keycamps and are running virtually the same programme as the original company.

Eurocamp

This company, started in 1972, has an approach very similar to Canvas Holidays and until 1981 stuck to the tried and tested formula of providing top-quality tents and equipment on sixty European sites. However, by popular request, the company started to offer caravans in its 1981 brochure. Eurocamp makes the point that its tents, over 25 sq m in size (272 sq ft) are twice the size of a conventional caravan. Tents are provided on sixty sites, mainly in France, but also in Germany, Switzerland, Italy and Austria.

Eurocamp offers direct travel to the continent from Eire.

In 1981 Eurocamp also branched into coach-based packages. Its Seasons Holidays are listed under coach holidays on page 000.

Inn-Tent

A comparative newcomer to the totally tent market, this is one of the few car-based rent-a-tent companies to belong to ABTA and to sell its holidays through over forty travel agents. The company, part of the Wallace Arnold coach organization, also accepts direct bookings. Inn-Tent, which includes refrigerators and sunshades with its equipment and has sprung single as well as double beds, has tents on one Italian and seven French sites, inland as well as on the Brittany, Mediterranean and Atlantic coasts. Campers who like to escape their fellow countrymen might be interested to learn that Inn-Tent has exclusive rights on five sites.

InterCamp

This company, formerly St Tropez Camping, offers two types of tent, one with a larger than usual living area and double bedroom. The company has tents on six sites, all in France, three on the Atlantic coast, two on the Mediterranean and one inland in the Ardèche.

Isle of Wight Holidays Ltd

This company, which specializes in self-catering holidays in the island, introduced rented tents for the first time in 1982. The tents are on a quiet country site a mile outside Shanklin.

Kellers of Balinsloe

Families living in Ireland can book camping packages direct with a company based in Galway. Kellers started offering this type of holiday four years ago and has tents on four French sites, all on the west coast.

Mocamps

This unique organization, originally set up in 1977 to provide strategically placed stops in fully furnished tents for campers *en route* for the Mediterranean, also offers long-term camping holidays. Of the seven sites available the company reckons that those at Monras, Montbazon and Sarlat are best for stays of up to a week for sightseeing and exploring. One of the plus points with Mocamps tents is that they all have electric lights. In 1982 the company started offering camping holidays at Fréjus on the Côte d'Azure.

Preston Travel

Lovers of the Channel Islands will be pleased to know that a company which has been providing holidays in this part of the world for twenty-five years recently set up a camping scheme. Preston Travel offers camping holidays in Jersey and Guernsey as well as in parts of Europe. For a Channel Islands holiday campers can either hire a fully furnished tent or take their own gear. Travel is either by sea or air.

CAR-BASED HOLIDAYS: TENTS AND CARAVANS

Carefree Camping

This company, started nine years ago, belongs more to the tent market, as of its twenty-five sites twenty have tents and five have caravans. Carefree, a pioneer of gas refrigerators in tents, is one of the companies to offer free holidays to infants in the low and mid seasons and to provide direct travel from Eire. Its sites, all French, are on the Atlantic and western Mediterranean coasts and in Brittany, Normandy and the Dordogne.

FreshFields

This company, an offshoot of Butlins, famous for pioneering holiday camps now known as holiday villages, has tent and caravan holidays in France and Spain. This side of the operation began in 1978 with thirteen French sites in Normandy, southern Brittany, on the Atlantic coast, the Camargue, the Auvergne and both the western Mediterranean and the Riviera. There is one Spanish site on the Costa Brava which is open until 26th September. Tents are available on three French sites only. FreshFields also offers boating holidays in France which could tie up with a week's camping. FreshFields has rented tents on two West Country sites.

International Camping Holidays.

This company, which now has more caravans than tents, began in 1974 and has tents on four Mediterranean sites. It offers four means of transport, car, train, air or coach, though the majority of campers use their own cars.

Keycamps

See under Ellerman Camping Holidays (page 52).

Leisuretime Holidays

One of the smaller companies that has held its own successfully for eight years, Leisuretime has both tents and caravans on two sites in Brittany, one in the Dordogne and one in the western Mediterranean. Leisuretime has linked up with a cruiser to provide six-day cruises down the Seine from Paris to Auxerre. So a fortnight's holiday could be half cruising, half camping.

Portland Camping

Another offshoot of a big holiday company Portland Camping, which began in 1982, has tents on twenty French sites – Brittany, the Vendée, the Dordogne, the western Mediterranean and the Riviera. The company supplies double and single sprung beds and refrigerators. Children under fourteen went free throughout the season on certain sites in 1982. There are some mobile homes.

Riviera Camping

This well established company (it is not at all connected with holiday companies with similar names), began eight years ago in the Riviera – where it has tents on one of the best sites in that part of the world – and plans to expand throughout France. Tents and caravans are already available in southern Brittany, on the Atlantic coast and in the Vendée. The equipment is good and in 1982 Riviera gave each tent a mains-run refrigerator. This is one of the companies to offer direct sailings from Rosslare to Le Havre or Cherbourg.

Solaire Holidays

As with a number of medium-sized companies, Solaire is a family-run concern and has been in the camping business for almost twelve years. Both tents and caravans are available and tents can be rented on twenty sites from Brittany to the Mediterranean in France and on one in Spain just south of Barcelona. Solaire has direct travel from Eire to the continent.

Sunsites

This company, which began in 1973, reckons that it is the largest concern of its kind to offer both tent and caravan holidays. There seems to be a growing demand for caravans in France, particularly on the Atlantic side of the country, with many people feeling that a caravan offers more protection against the elements. Twenty of the Sunsites camps from Normandy to the Mediterranean offer tents.

COACH-BASED CAMPING HOLIDAYS

As with the car-based holidays there is something available for everyone, so read the brochures carefully, to find the best holiday to suit you.

Some coach-based holidays are aimed at families who like plenty of entertainment and provide special clubs for children, arrange sporting activities, lay on excursions and organize parties and competitions. Sometimes companies providing this kind of holiday take over a complete site and run a holiday village just for their own clients. Other coach-based companies take tents on sites within walking distance of the nearest town and leave clients to make their own amusements; these sites can be either quiet or very lively. Some organizations will make arrangements for campers to hire cars. Equally, if this is not provided you can either make your own enquiries about car hire or investigate local bus and train times for the days when you want to make excursions away from the camp.

Coach/camp companies vary a great deal in the way in which they charge for their holidays, and it is therefore impossible to give an average or typical price for a fourteen-day package. Coach journeys, particularly those to the Mediterranean, can be long and tiresome. Check the type of coach used and the facilities offered on board; some have toilets, some provide coffee machines, some put on film shows and most have air conditioning. Find out how many drivers there are; most of the journeys are non-stop, and it takes just under twenty-four hours to travel from London to the Mediterranean. All European countries have their own as well as Common Market safety rules for coaches. Briefly, a driver cannot be at the wheel for more than four hours at a stretch and must not drive for more than eight hours a day. Drivers should have at least ten hours' break away from the coach in every twenty-four hour period. Some coach companies pick up and exchange drivers as they drive through France. Some companies take their own coaches across the Channel, others pick up a coach on the other side. In the interests of safety and comfort it is worth looking into the details of the coach journey. For instance, look at departure times: it is sometimes possible to avoid a long hot daytime drive on the continent. If you live outside London check whether the company that interests you has provincial pick-up points.

Unlike most car-based holiday concerns, coach/camping companies do not offer holidays at a completely inclusive price. Often the basic charge includes transport and a furnished tent with cooking utensils and insurance generally as extras. The following companies are listed alphabetically.

Averoy Travel Ltd

This company, which also has caravans, provides well-furnished tents on four sites in the French Riviera and on one on the Spanish Costa Brava. The holidays are aimed at people who like to organize their own time: individual excursions can easily be made from all the sites. There are no extra charges for equipment or gas, and continental breakfast is included in the price. However, a refundable deposit of £20 per tent is required. Coaches start from London, Leeds, Liverpool, Manchester and Birmingham.

Berkeley Holidays

This company, started seven years ago, has tents and caravans on sites in Brittany, the south of France and Spain. It is mainly coach-based but also provides self-drive and fly/camp holidays. The coach journey can include an overnight stop in Paris with a day off for sightseeing. Tents are fully furnished, and there are no extra charges, but you must bring your own sleeping bags and cutlery. Main coach departures are from London, Manchester and Birmingham, with reduced rail fares from other parts of the country to the pick-up points.

Camping Club of the Mediterranean

This company, now in its seventh year, specializes in Mediterranean sites: it owns one of the three French sites on which it has tents and has total control over the other two. Travel is from London's Victoria (though there is one self-drive holiday on offer). In the case of the coach-based holidays, which cross the Channel by hovercraft, a mini-bus provides transport into the nearest town, and a coach is available for excursions. Cooking packs are extra, about £20 for a two week holiday. Camping Club holidays can be booked through a number of travel agencies.

Club Cantabrica

A well-established company that has been going for eight years, Club Cantabrica has tents, caravans and bungalows in France, Spain, Italy and Greece. All equipment, except for cutlery and sleeping bags is included. There are a number of pick-ups in provincial towns; all the coaches, owned directly by the company, are equipped with toilets and a coffee bar, and films can be screened on board. In 1982 the company started fly/camp holidays in Italy and Corfu.

Halcyon Summer Holidays

This company, which has air and coach holidays, provides everything in its camping pack except cutlery and has been in existence for thirteen years. It is one of the few companies to offer camping holidays in Corfu. Other sites are in Spain, the south of France, the Italian Riviera, Greece and the Algarve.

Holiday Adventure

This company specializes in adventure holidays to Spain, Andorra, Morocco and Israel. It also offers beach camping in the South of France and Spain and watersports – windsurfing, scuba diving and so on – in the Mediterranean. It is a small company catering for both families and singles. Those travelling solo should be prepared to share a tent. Coach departures from London, Manchester, Leeds, Leicester and Hemel Hempstead.

Nat Holidays

This organization, a member of ABTA, aims its holidays mainly at families who enjoy having activities laid on and has a special free day-care service and play area for children between four and eleven years old. Nat also runs camping holidays for young people and couples and, as well as coach packages, provides air travel or makes arrangements for clients to take their own cars to the camp site. The company has been in operation for fourteen years and gets most of its customers through travel agents. Tents are on sites in France, Spain, Greece, Austria, Italy, Portugal and Switzerland, and, as well as 'static' holidays, Nat offers camping tours. Coach departures are from London, Bristol, Liverpool, Manchester, Leeds, Newcastle, Swansea and Glasgow, but not all holidays start from all eight cities, so check before you book. Cooking packs, cool boxes and lanterns can be hired at an additional charge; otherwise the tent is fully furnished. Tent holidays, fly/camp in Greece for the under thirties were started by Nat in 1982. In 1982 Nat took over the Mediterranean holiday village at Cap d'Agde previously run by Sunsaver.

Seasons Holidays

This off-shoot of the experienced car-based rent-a-tent company Eurocamp has linked up with coach operators Wallace Arnold to provide family camping holidays at four four-star sites on the French Mediterranean. All equipment is included. Coach departures are from London, Leeds, Birmingham, Manchester and Dover, and Seasons states clearly in its brochure that its coaches operate with a team of four experienced British drivers.

Solmer Travel Ltd

This small company, which has been in operation for eight years, specializes in camping holidays to Corsica. Tents are on a three-star site outside Calvi, a fishing port on the north-west of the island. Both the beach and the town are within easy walking distance of the site. The cost includes all equipment except cutlery and sleeping bags. Campers can either fly or travel overland by coach across France and take the six-hour ferry to Corsica.

Tentrek Holidays

This company, in its twelfth year and a member of ABTA, has now moved out of the totally young person's market and caters for all campers. Coach/camp holidays are to Brittany, the South of France, Italy, Yugoslavia and Spain with self-drive holidays to Brittany and the South of France. Cooking packs cost £10.75 for a ten-day holiday and £15.75 for a seventeen-day holiday. Lanterns and ice boxes cost extra. Both small (two to three people) and large (up to six people) size tents are available. Departures, usually from National Express pick-up points, are from a number of provincial cities as well as London. Self-drive holidays are also available.

OTHER ORGANIZATIONS OFFERING RENTED TENTS

A growing number of organizations not generally associated with camping has started to offer rented tents as part of a general holiday programme. Twickenham Travel for example, known for its unusual and adventurous holidays, has started to offer fly/drive/camp packages to Iceland and fly/drive or bus/camp holidays to Israel, while Ventura Holidays, which has been dealing in direct-sell villas and apartments in Greece and the surrounding islands for eleven years, now also offers beach camping holidays, mainly for the young, on Corfu and Crete. That pioneer of travel, Thomas Cook, has an overland camping trip to Russia and

Scandinavia and one to North Africa in its *Searcher* brochure.

Ladbroke, a name not normally associated with camping, now offers rent-a-tent holidays in Cornwall, Wales and the Isle of Wight. Page & Moy Ltd, who link up with the TV Times Travel Service, have coach-based camping holidays in the South of France.

The ferry companies too have thrown themselves into camping, with many linking up with rent-a-tent operators or putting their own packages together. In its *Continental Motoring Holidays* brochure Sealink tied up with Mocamps for overnight stops in 1982. The French Travel Service has also joined with Sealink to include car-based holidays in its *Les Vacances Vertes* brochure. The fully furnished tents are on a site at Najac, south of the Dordogne and on a farm in the Rouergue. The farm site is run in conjunction with l'Association Nationale du Camping en Ferme d'Accueil (mentioned in Chapter 3), an organization formed to promote friendship between country and town people. The high season cost for a camping package on the farm, including cross Channel transport, came to just under £240 for a family of four in 1982. Tents, either two- or four-berth, are equipped with essentials, but gas is not provided, and there are no couriers. However, the sites in this brochure sound ideal for those who want to avoid the intensely camped areas of France.

Brittany Ferries, Townsend Thoresen and P&O Ferries offer camping packages in their ferry brochures. A holiday centre, developed in conjunction with Brittany Ferries at Le Cleuziou in northern Brittany, provides a four-star site in the grounds of a thirteenth-century manor house set in seventeen acres of parkland. The manor house is open to the public and campers may use many of the facilities provided, including the heated swimming pool, the indoor games and television rooms and the bar and may attend the evening dances and discos. Although campers do not have to book with Brittany Ferries to use the site, those who do get a 25 percent discount if they stay for three nights or more.

Townsend Thoresen has a holiday village on the Belgian coast at De Haan, about midway between the ports of Ostend and Zeebrugge. Both furnished four- and six-berth tents as well as chalets are on offer. The site, which is very flat and has a heated outdoor swimming pool and a laundrette, might be a good proposition for a family with small children who do not want to drive very far, but who just want to cross the Channel. In the 1982 high season a tent for four cost £16 a night for up to six nights and £15 a night for seven or more nights. All rent-a-tent bookings have to be made in conjunction with car ferry reservations, but those with their own equipment can book a pitch on the site.

Fully furnished tents in six different coastal regions of France are offered in the *P&O Auto-Stay* brochure. In 1982 an inclusive holiday for two adults and two children cost from just over £400.

The ferries that cross the North Sea are also waking up to the potential of camping, with DFDS (UK) Ltd helping those with their own equipment. In its *Scandinavian Summer Holidays* DFDS offers camping cheque cards or vouchers as part of a camping package. Each camping cheque entitles up to five people, with their tent and their car, to spend a night at any site in Sweden, Norway or Finland. In 1982 a family of four paid just over £300 for a seven-day holiday in Scandinavia using these cheques. This cost included the return sea passage, an economy class cabin and the cheques, which are collected on the ferry boat. This holiday may not seem very long when the journeys there and back take twenty-four hours each way, but extra camping cheques, starting at £3.50 each, are obtainable. So a longer holiday can be planned, and campers could use the scheme to visit all three Scandinavian countries in one holiday if they had the time, inclination and money.

A similar deal is offered in the *Danish Seaways* brochure, also put out by DFDS. This time the camping cheques cover staying on a selection of twelve top-grade sites in Denmark, once again for those with their own equipment. In 1982 a family of four paid £340 for a ten-day holiday. This included return sea passage, an economy class cabin and seven camping cheques. Additional cheques, to extend the holiday, are available. Campers in Denmark should remember that a camping carnet is essential.

Finally, the Fred. Olsen Line, now also part of DFDS, has camping cheque holidays in its *Norway 82* brochure. The scheme, covering 600 camp sites, is for ten days, which can be extended. High season prices for four: £440. In its 1982 *Iceland* brochure Fred. Olsen Travel had one and two week camping safaris in Iceland with prices starting at £385 per person. This included return flight from London to Reykjavik and all meals and accommodation on the safari. Both holidays were in the north-west highland region of Iceland, with the coach-based safari going off the beaten tracks and into the interior of the country. Company staff prepare meals and pitch and take down the tents.

Even the railways have muscled in on the act, and, in the *France '82* brochure issued by the French Travel Service, British Rail and French Rail have cooperated to offer a number of camping packages. Once children are old enough to manage a suitcase apiece there is a good deal to be said for a rail-based camping holiday, particularly if a long journey is involved. Train departures can sometimes be more flexible than coach departures, and a journey by train, when passengers can move around freely and where tables can provide space for children's games or drawing books, can often be less tiring than a coach or car journey. Moreover, today's children, not generally accustomed to trains, are often enchanted by this means of transport, with meals *en route*, either in the dining car or bought from sandwich-selling men at stations, all adding to the fun of the holiday.

Of the fifteen camping holidays listed in the *France '82* brochure not all include the use of a fully furnished tent; with some you have to take your own gear and while this may not be too difficult for single people it is not very practical for a family. However, fully furnished rented tents are available in Brittany, the Dordogne and Corsica. In 1982 a family of four taking a ten-day high season fully furnished tent in Brittany paid £484 for their holiday. This included rail travel from any main line station in Great Britain – quite a saving this – to La Baule. Sleeping bags were included in this particular holiday, so campers had to bring only the liners.

Finally, Rentatent, the well-known camping equipment hire company, has started providing fully furnished tents on a camping park in Jersey. Both drive/camp and fly/camp packages are on offer.

Hiring of camping packs: who offers what

It looks as though only big concerns are involved in the hiring out of camping packs nowadays as out of the twelve companies contacted when this book was being compiled only three replied. However, it might be worth checking in the yellow pages to see what is available locally. Finding a reliable company to hand makes collection and delivery easy and does mean that you can get the gear a couple of days before the holiday to enable you to test it out in the garden if you wish. Remember though to get enquiries under way early in the year; there will inevitably be heavy bookings for equipment during July and August.

So, for families who want the freedom of being able to camp where they wish without the financial outlay involved in buying their own gear the major companies that can supply all the equipment are listed alphabetically below. Remember to book what you need well in advance and to clean the equipment before returning it. Rentatent, who sell off all their equipment at the end of each season, speak very highly of the condition in which camping packs are returned.

The Automobile Association

This organization has been in the camping hire business for five years and reckons that its packs appeal to first-time campers. A minimum of twenty-eight days' notice is required to hire a pack. A family of four will pay in the region of £104 for a fortnight's pack. This includes insurance and VAT. The pack contains a tent, a groundsheet, a two-burner stove, with grill and stand, gas, a table, four campbeds, four chairs and a gas lantern, complete with gas cylinder. Roof racks are available for hire but cost extra with a minimum hire period of five days. The AA, which reckons that each of its packs has a retail value of around £600, says that hiring saves the holidaymaker about £100 on the cost of renting a fully furnished tent. Packs have to be collected from the AA's hire-services depot at Dover. This organization also provides an Argosy inclusive pack which includes camping equipment, ferry bookings and AA five-star insurance. In 1982 the AA introduced trailer tent hire. Details from the Dover office.

Blacks Camping and Leisure

This company hires out packs from its London office and also provides, at substantial discount, packs to customers crossing the Channel via Sealink ferries. Either ridge or frame tents, the largest big enough to sleep six, are available, with twenty items, including a roof rack, on offer. A family of four could expect to pay under £100 for a four-berth tent, a groundsheet, campbeds, chairs, a table, a cooker, with stand and gas and a lantern. This would be a fortnight's hire. Campers going to the Mediterranean might consider adding a cool box at 24p a day and a larder for the same price.

Rentatent

This company has three depots, both for renting and sales, in Wembley, Wakefield and Manchester. Over forty items can be hired singly, but there is a reduced rate for a package deal. A family of four would pay between £57 and £76 (depending on the season) for a fortnight's hire of a pack consisting of a tent, a folding table, two folding armchairs, two large stools, crockery, cutlery, a cooker with grill, a kitchen unit, a gas cylinder, a kettle and pans, two washing up bowls, a 9 l (2 gal) water carrier, one double and two single airbeds, a foot inflator and a tent light which runs off the car battery.

Names and addresses

Canvas Holidays,
Bull Plain,
Hertford,
Herts SG14 1DY.

Ellerman Camping Holidays,
73-74 High Holborn,
London WC1V 6LS.

Eurocamp Travel Ltd,
Edmundson House,
Tatton Street,
Knutsford,
Cheshire WA16 6BG.

Inn-Tent Ltd,
26 Bank Street,
Wetherby,
West Yorkshire LS22 4NQ.

InterCamp,
4 Greenwood Avenue,
Parkstone,
Poole,
Dorset.

Isle of Wight Holidays,
Wight House,
28 Luccombe Road,
Shanklin,
Isle of Wight PO37 6RR.

Kellers of Ballinasloe Ltd,
Main Street,
Ballinasloe,
Galway,
Eire.

Mocamps Ltd,
38-40 High Street,
Green Street Green,
Orpington,
Kent BR6 6BJ.

Preston Travel,
4 Dollis Park,
London N3 1JU.

Carefree Camping Ltd,
41-43 Stephyns Chambers,
Bank Court,
Hemel Hempstead,
Herts HP1 1DG.

FreshField Holidays,
Freepost,
PO Box 20,
Cirencester,
Gloucestershire GL7 1RS.

International Camping Holidays,
14 Kelvinbrook,
Hurst Park,
West Molesey,
Surrey KT8 9RZ.

Leisuretime Holidays (France) Ltd,
276 Monument Road,
Birmingham B16 8XF.

Portland Camping,
65 Bolsover Street,
London W1P 7ML.

Riviera Camping Ltd,
12 Marston Lane,
Rolleston-on-Dove,
Staffs DE13 9BH.

Solaire Holidays,
The Coach House,
241 Hagley Road,
Edgbaston,
Birmingham B16 9RR.

Sunsites Ltd,
1 South Street,
Dorking,
Surrey RH4 2DY.

Coach-based camping holidays are also mainly direct sell, though some companies do work through travel agents. However, in the majority of cases you will have to send away for a brochure.

Averoy Travel Ltd,
Averoy House,
Market Street,
Altrincham,
Cheshire.

Holiday Adventure Ltd,
The White House,
51 Marlowes,
Hemel Hempstead,
Herts.

Berkeley Holidays,
The Square,
Holmes Chapel,
Cheshire CW4 7AH.

Nat Holidays Ltd,
1-5 Standard Road,
London NW 10.

**Camping Club of the
Mediterranean Ltd,**
152 Holland Park Avenue,
London W11.

Seasons Holidays Ltd,
Edmundson House,
Tatton Street,
Knutsford,
Cheshire WA16 6BG.

Club Cantabrica Holidays Ltd,
2-6 Verulam Road,
St Albans,
Herts AL3 4DD.

Solmer Travel,
100 Palewell Park,
London SW14.

Tentrek,
152 Maidstone Road,
Ruxley Corner,
Sidcup,
Kent DA14 5HS.

Halcyon Summer Holidays,
Halcyon House,
Wincolmlee,
Hull HU2 8HT.

Companies only indirectly connected with camping or offering camping holidays to a limited market:

Sunsport and Suntoppers are part of the PGL Group.
PGL Holidays,
2/5 Market Place,
Ross-on-Wye HR9 5LD.

Twickenham Travel Ltd,
84 Hampton Road,
Twickenham,
Middlesex TW2 5QS.

Sealink Ltd,
163 Eversholt Street,
London NW1 1BG.

The French Travel Service,
Francis House,
Francis Street,
London SW1P 1DE.

Ventura Holidays,
279 South Road,
Sheffield S6 3TA.

Searcher Adventure Travel,
Thomas Cook Ltd,
PO Box 36,
Peterborough PE3 6SB.

Ladbroke Holidays,
PO Box 137,
Millbuck House,
Clarendon Road,
Watford WD1 1DN.

Page & Moy Ltd,
136-140 London Road,
Leicester LE2 1EN.

Brittany Ferries,
Milbay Docks,
Plymouth PL1 3EF.

Townsend Thoresen,
Russell Street,
Dover,
Kent CT16 1OB.

P&O Ferrytours,
Arundel Towers,
Portland Terrace,
Southampton SO9 4AE.

For DFDS Tor Line, Danish Seaways and Fred. Olsen brochures write to:
DFDS(UK) Ltd,
Latham House,
16 Minories,
London EC3N 1AN.

AA Hire Service,
Snargate Street,
Dover,
Kent CT17 9XA.

Rentatent,
Twitch Hill,
Horbury,
Wakefield WF4 6LZ.

Blacks Camping & Leisure Ltd,
10/11 Catford Broadway,
London SE6 4SP.

Rentatent,
40 Ducie Street,
Manchester M1 2JN.

Rentatent,
Third Way,
Wembley Hill Trading Estate,
Wembley HA9 0TE.

3
Choosing the Right Site

Choosing the right site for longer than an overnight stop is crucial to the success of a camping holiday. As with villas, apartments, holiday houses or hotels, it pays to do your homework thoroughly beforehand, reading site guides with an eye to detail and using two or three different sources to try to build up an overall picture.

Nowadays, camping, particularly with big family-sized frame tents, has to take place on formal sites, for the activity has grown so much in popularity, particularly over the past ten years, that it has become virtually impossible to camp 'wild', in other words, just where you want to; most countries discourage this practice, and some actually forbid it. In that most over-camped part of Europe, the Var region of the French Mediterranean, there are annual clashes between the authorities and the *campeurs sauvages* who, unable to get on to a site pitch their tents on the roadside, in fields, or anywhere they can find space.

In Britain it is still possible to camp 'wild', usually in the more remote mountain areas, and on the whole those who do camp like this tend to be loners with ridge tents rather than families with big frame tents. Camping on open ground, as opposed to formal camp sites, is allowed in the less crowded countries of northern Europe, notably Sweden and Iceland.

However, although camping wild may have a romantic appeal, sites with their sanitary arrangements, shops, safe drinking-water supplies, security guards, access to medical aid and even church on Sunday are far better for families. Stealing from campers is a minor industry in parts of Europe and those who camp wild do so at their peril – even physical attacks are not uncommon in certain southern regions.

Moreover, organized sites have eliminated many of the other difficulties encountered when camping wild. On a good site, pitches will have been levelled, unnecessary undergrowth cleared away, marshy land drained and, in some cases, where the ground is exposed, trees will have been planted. So if camping on an organized site seems a little tame, it does at least help to make life under canvas more comfortable and does remove some of the unseen difficulties that sometimes only become apparent after a tent has been pitched wild.

To find the right site, campers using their own gear should consult a selection of the dozen or so guides (available from bookshops and some camping shops), approximately half of which list sites in the British Isles and half of which cover the continent.

Added to these is the information put out by the British, Scottish, Northern Ireland and Wales Tourist Boards, the regional tourist boards and the tourist offices in individual towns. The London-based tourist offices of European countries where camping is popular, or is becoming more popular, will generally supply lists of camp sites. These offices also send out, when requested, excellent background information on what their country has to offer tourists in general. After all, campers are holiday-makers as much as any other tourist – they just live under a canvas instead of a tiled roof. Like any other holidaymakers they want to explore new surroundings, try unusual restaurants, visit museums, art galleries, cathedrals and churches, go shopping and learn something of the background of the country they are visiting.

When choosing a site from the guides look out for the words 'park' or 'caravan site'. The term 'park' is becoming more popular with site owners in an effort to get away from the slightly jokey image of the word 'camp'; it also often implies that static caravans, let out as holiday homes, occupy a fair proportion of the site. The atmosphere on this type of site is totally different from that on a site where tents predominate, so check the descriptions a site gives of itself, what is the proportion of tents to caravans and whether the caravans are touring or static. Remember also that a number of sites, particularly those open all the year round, vary their intake, with many more caravans turning up in the winter than tents. The really big parks of static vans tend to be in very popular holiday areas such as Cornwall. Quiet inland sites that are 'parks' have a very different atmosphere.

Symbols and ratings

With a bit of practice it is fairly easy to understand the symbols used in the guide books. Many, such as the sign for a shop, swimming pool, a restaurant or 'dogs not allowed', seem to be universal.

Careful reading of the symbols lessens the chance of picking the wrong site. Symbols in the good guides will tell you whether there are marked-out individual pitches or whether campers just choose their own spot; they will indicate whether a site is shady and whether it is level all over or sloping in parts. The symbols will also tell you about hot showers, shopping and washing facilities, and amusements and distractions. The more symbols, the better you are able to build up a good mental image of the site. One of the best guides around, the Michelin Guide to French sites, uses forty-four symbols.

It is, of course, harder to gauge the 'feel' of a site from a guide, although it is possible to pick up clues from the hard facts given. Five or six sites, all fairly close together in a popular seaside resort, for example, are not likely to be havens of peace. However, two books, the AA's *Camping and Caravanning in Britain* and the Michelin *Camping, Caravanning France*, give ratings as well as using symbols and both guides go a step further and try to give an idea of atmosphere. Remember, however, that ratings indicate the overall quality of facilities and that a site with a high rating is not necessarily the best in every way, just as a lower rating does not mean lower standards but simply more modest equipment. Most top-rating sites have excellent facilities, plenty of showers, tiled and clean where the hot water never runs cold, a well-stocked shop, washing and drying machines, an excellent restaurant and possibly a heated swimming pool. This can often go hand in hand with well-organized social activities, bingo sessions, old-time dancing, discos or film shows for the evenings and a constant stream of entertainment for children and adults during the day. Some families, those with small children who need to be amused or who need to use washing and drying machines, or families who like an organized social life, will enjoy all the activity and bustle such sites offer; others might find such a cheerfully noisy site not at all to their liking. Campers looking for peace and quiet might do better to go for lower ratings and for sites far away from popular areas.

Other guides for choosing a site

Apart from mastering the symbols and interpreting the ratings in guide books, choosing a site can be difficult from another point of view for family campers – trying to please everyone, a near impossible task. When children are small and do not have much say in the matter beyond a preference for seaside holidays, the choice is not too difficult. As they get older and begin to have views on what type of site they enjoy, the final choice has to be negotiated rather than arbitrarily decided by the parents. At this stage a compromise works best: a couple of days at a quiet site for the benefit of the adults in the party, followed by a spell at a 'lively' site, i.e. one with a disco or other forms of teenage entertainment.

Finally, it is still possible to make a visual assessment of the site on arrival and change your mind if you do not like what you see, provided that you have not reserved a pitch in advance. You must, of course, allow enough time to go elsewhere if you intend to rely on this method of selecting a site. When you arrive, try to park a little way from the reception area while you make your decision. Once in the office it is pretty hard to say you have changed your mind about booking in! You can always ask the opinion of people already camping at a site before committing yourself.

If you have the nerve, and plenty of people do, walk in and inspect the toilet block before booking in – it makes sense, particularly if you are planning a stay for longer than a couple of days. As well as being clean, lavatories, wash basins and showers should be well maintained and in good condition. Look at the clothes-washing facilities: check whether separate sinks are provided and if there are communal washing lines and where they are positioned. Look at the dish-washing sinks: these, standard on the continent, are now becoming more commonplace in England. Ideally they should be free from scraps of food, but untidiness here is more the fault of the careless camper than the site proprietor.

Camp sites, very much like hotels or restaurants, depend to a large extent on the personality of the owner or warden for their atmosphere. A well-run site will have neatly cut grass and well-maintained grounds, the boundary fence will be in a good state of repair and the dustbins sturdy and not overflowing, while charges and rules will be clearly displayed at the front of the office. Look for tents neatly laid out rather than pitched higgledy-piggledy. Some sites, even with only the basic essentials, have a very pleasant atmosphere; others, highly sophisticated, can be over-organized with many admonishing notices around and an atmosphere of too much discipline and not enough relaxation.

For future reference it is well worth making brief notes on each camp either alongside the entry in the guide book or in a special camping notebook.

Reservations

The camping season is short, generally from Easter to September, although some sites, both here and abroad, stay open all year. Camping, like all other holidays, reaches its peak in the school summer break, so anyone thinking of camping between mid-July and the end of August should consider booking. It is also worth making reservations if you are considering camping in England over the popular Easter, spring and summer bank holiday weekends.

BOOKING IN ENGLAND

There are two schools of thought on booking pitches in this country: some people never do because they feel it will restrict them; others would never dream of driving off without having booked first.

On the booking front, there can be hazards. Even if you have booked, try to arrive at the site early, or you could find that 'casual' campers who have turned up before you have been allocated the best pitches. You can, if you know a site well and particularly if it has pitches marked out, ask for a certain spot to be reserved for you, but not many people, unless they return time and time again to the same site, have this kind of knowledge.

Another point to bear in mind is that there is no overall approach to reservations. Some sites actively discourage booking while others encourage it, but only at certain times, such as the spring or August bank holiday weekends. Sites also vary in the way they treat reservations. Some are very exact and like to be given certain dates and ask for a minimum number of days to be booked, often a week. They expect quite a hefty deposit and often a booking fee and will not refund any money if you have to leave early. Other sites are much more casual, need only a token deposit and allow you to extend your stay if you wish. Sites that do not have marked-out pitches often accept a booking made in advance merely as guaranteeing entry to the site: you then find your own pitch, hence the importance of turning up early in the afternoon. Some campsite guide books do not comment on reservation rules because they vary so much from camp to camp, but others do their best to indicate the preferences of individual sites.

CONTINENTAL RESERVATIONS

Making reservations for continental sites can be a little more tricky than booking for a British one. But, as always when there is a gap in the market, someone has stepped in to fill it. For those unsure of their ability to make their own continental reservations there are a number of organizations willing to take over the problem.

Camp Resa, an organization based in Paris, will make bookings for campers with their own gear on some 150 sites in France, Spain and Greece. The company issues an annual sheet listing the sites, their location, classification and a number of other details. Once again, reservations are not accepted for less than a week. Prospective campers have to send off the booking form together with a deposit of 300 French francs (around £30), plus a reservation fee of 95 French francs. The 300 francs will be deducted from the total bill at the end of your stay.

Another organization working from the same Paris address, Campexel, offers reservations on any of a chain of nineteen sites linked together by a charter guaranteeing the holidaymaker 'dependability and quality'. Campexel, also asks for a deposit of 300 francs and a reservation fee of 50 francs. As with the Resa scheme, when the booking has been made on your behalf you receive written confirmation together with further details of the site. The little booklet put out by Campexel has site location maps and fairly detailed information on the sites in the scheme, the majority of which are in Brittany and on the Mediterranean coast.

Finally, a new organization, Camping and Caravanning on the Farm, Camping Caravanning en Ferme d'Accueil, offers good low-cost camping holidays on farms. There are never more than six tents or caravans, or twenty-five people, allowed on each farm site, adequate toilet facilities have to be provided, and it has to be possible for campers to buy fresh produce from the farm. At present the scheme operates only in the Midi-Pyrenees region of France and is backed by a charter setting out the rules which members offering camping facilities must observe. There is an office in each of the four *départements* which deals with bookings, provides background information and organizes local entertainments. To give an idea of charges, in 1982 a family of four with its own equipment paid around £2.50 per person per week. Write for general background information and a 1983 price list, printed in English. Remember to include a self-addressed envelope and an international reply coupon. This coupon, obtainable from any post office, costs 30p and is a form of international postage stamp. (Address on page 85.)

A number of farms included in the *French Farm and Village Holiday Guide*, published by McCarta Ltd, allow camping on their land. The guide should be available from bookshops from January onwards and in 1982 cost £3.50. The name and address of each farm is given in the book, as well as a description and a photograph of the farmhouse. You make your own bookings, either direct with the farmer or through the regional booking service. Once again, include an international reply coupon and a self-addressed envelope with your letter. A sample booking form is given in the guide.

Those independent enough to make their own reservations – not too difficult if you use the standard letter given on page 89 – will need one of the European camp site guides for names and addresses. Do not assume that the addresses given in these guides are incomplete because they look short; remember that each must be preceded by 'The Proprietor' and followed by the actual name of the camp site, the postal code, the town or village and finally the name of the country.

The Michelin Guide, which covers only France, is very clear in its indication of a site's attitude to booking. The situation there is very much as in England: some sites do not accept advance bookings, others regard them as practically obligatory, while others do not mind if you book or not, but probably would prefer you to do so in the peak season.

The AA's *Camping and Caravanning in Europe* recommends that campers book for the peak period, but does not indicate which sites will accept bookings. The best course of action in this case is to send a standard booking letter to the site of your choice with a self-addressed envelope and international reply coupon and hope for the best.

However, before you make your continental reservation you will need to study the available camp-site guides carefully. Here is a brief description of those generally available. The prices quoted are for the 1982 guides and these are subject to change. Guides are usually published annually: some come out before Christmas, some early in the New Year, and by March there should be enough available for you to make a selection from which to compare sites.

Camp-site guides: Great Britain

Useful though these guides are, it should be stated that a number of British sites are so well established that the proprietors do not apply for inclusion in any guide. Prices quoted are for 1982 copies.

CAMPING AND CARAVANNING IN BRITAIN

Produced by the AA at £2.75, this is the most expensive but the most comprehensive guide on the market and gives very detailed information on some nine hundred and fifty camps. Although there are over two thousand sites in Britain, the AA reckons that fewer than a thousand of those which apply for inclusion in the guide come up to its standards.

Contrary to the view held by many people, the guide is not 'run through a computer' but is compiled on an inspection basis. Inclusion in the guide does not mean automatic re-entry the following year if the standard of facilities on a site has dropped. The AA's team of thirty inspectors, who also check hotels, guest houses, farmhouses and other forms of accommodation, keeps an annual eye on sites already in the guide. Proprietors wishing to be included have to go through standard procedure, first filling in a four-page questionnaire then, if this makes the grade, being visited by inspectors, and finally having their application considered by a committee.

The guide uses just under sixty symbols and abbreviations, which is why it is a good idea to familiarize yourself with it before leaving home. Camp sites are listed alphabetically, there are eight pages of maps at the back of the book giving site locations, and where necessary sketch maps are given in the text. A big plus with the guide is that, as well as giving full details of each site, it also provides a six-figure map reference based on the national grid and the number of the relevant Ordnance Survey map. For it is a feature of most camp sites, unlike hotels or guest houses, that they are not always easily accessible, so adequate map references are important. The book lists sites in England, Wales, Scotland, the Channel Islands and the Isle of Man.

A separate book, *Ireland – Where to go, What to do*, also published by the AA (at £2.50), lists camp sites for the whole of the country as well as a good deal of other information helpful to holidaymakers, such as a list of castles, houses and gardens open to the public and details of the surprisingly large number of forest parks (almost three hundred). This is published annually in July.

RAC CAMPING AND CARAVANNING SITES

There are three books altogether, priced at 75p each. These list nearly one thousand sites in England, Scotland and Wales inspected by the RAC.

CAMPING SITES IN BRITAIN

Costing £1.40, this is produced by *Camping* magazine and contains a list of more than fifteen hundred sites ranging from luxurious holiday centres to modestly equipped farms. It is aimed at campers rather than caravanners.

Camps are listed by county for England, Scotland and Wales, and Irish sites are listed alphabetically. More than fifty symbols are used and there is no grading of sites. Direction of how to reach each site is given in the text. A site-location map would be useful, as most people's geography, even of their own country, is hazy.

The publishers say they send out questionnaires to camps who have not previously been in the guide and ask existing entries to verify details. Those who do not reply are dropped.

PRACTICAL CAMPER'S SITES GUIDE

This, costing £1.25, is another publication put out by a monthly magazine. It lists over one thousand sites, county by county, in England, Wales, Scotland, the Scilly Isles, the Isle of Man, the Channel Islands and Northern Ireland. A full description is given of each site, but no symbols are used and no grading is given. Once again, although adequate instructions are given in the text for reaching camps, there is no site-reference map in the book.

CADE'S CAMPING SITE GUIDE

Brought out by Marwain Publishing and listing fifteen hundred camp sites in England, Wales and Scotland, county by county, this costs £1.10. Thirty-four symbols are used. Since 1981 the guide, which does not have a grading system and which relies on information sent in by site owners, has included information on camps which have facilities for the disabled. Site owners are contacted each year to verify information. There is a special West Country edition costing 80p.

LETTS GUIDE: CARAVAN AND CAMP SITES IN BRITAIN

Costing £1.95, this guide lists over two thousand sites in England, Scotland and Wales, grouping them into sixteen regions. This guide manages to use only ten symbols (which simplifies reading), gives the Ordnance Survey grid number, and stars those sites which have confirmed that the information about them in the guide is correct. There is a brief description of each region, including the names of towns with tourist offices and a map of the region showing the principal roads. There is no site-location map.

GOOD CAMPS GUIDE

This guide, by Alan Rogers published by Deneway Guides and costing £1.10, lists only those sites in England, Scotland and Wales that have been visited and are considered good by the author. Mr Rogers starts his book with sites in Cornwall and works his way round the country but recommends that readers consult the site-location map in the middle of the book to identify areas. He gives an excellent personal account of each site he has visited, as well as details of the equipment, and comments on any unusual features. He tries whenever possible to give details of reservations and always quotes the Ordnance Survey map reference. Well thought-out, with attention to the kind of detail useful to families, its use of personal comments in place of symbols makes this a very easy guide to assimilate.

THE CAMPING AND CARAVANNING CLUB

This organization celebrated its eightieth birthday in 1981. It has a national network of sites, most of which are reserved for members only. If you plan to camp in England, or take weekend breaks in this country, it may be worth joining the club as its sites cover all types of holiday area from the seaside to places of outstanding natural beauty, from camps in the depth of the country to sites close to towns. Membership runs from the beginning of November to the end of the following October and costs an initial £11.50, which includes a membership fee. Thereafter the annual subscription is £10.00. This is quite generous in that it covers all children under eighteen and one adult member of the family.

Members receive the club handbook which, as well as listing in great detail the club sites, gives information of over two thousand five hundred commercial and farm sites in England, Scotland, Wales, the Channel Islands, and both Northern Ireland and Eire. The guide is used in conjunction with an excellent site-location sheet map, specially prepared for the club by the Ordnance Survey.

Also available to members is a monthly magazine, and they may make use of the information service, which answers questions on camping and caravanning, and the foreign touring service. The club has thirteen regions, consequently many events and social occasions are arranged at local level.

WHERE TO STAY

Published by the English Tourist Board, this costs £2.50 and includes over sixty pages of names and addresses of camp sites and their charges along with information on all forms of self-catering holidays in England. All the sites mentioned are registered with the English Tourist Board, and the proprietors have agreed to abide by the Board's code of conduct. Most have been inspected.

Also listed in this main guide are the names and addresses of the twelve regional tourist boards (these are also given on page 85), each of which produces its own *Where to Stay*, most costing £1; the West Country version however costs £1.10. The guides should be available from most bookshops from January onwards. If you order them from the relevant tourist board include an extra 30p for packing and postage. As well as giving camp-site information, each regional guide lists the names and addresses of tourist information centres in individual towns – most useful as these local centres (over 470 of them throughout England) can often provide up-to-the minute information on site vacancies. Each tourist board produces a sheet listing all its publications and their prices; best to get the sheet of the region that interests you before ordering any books.

In 1979 the English Tourist Board began a Camping and Caravanning Advisory Service to encourage advance booking. The relevant regional tourist board can provide details of the service and the telephone numbers of the special centres. By 1982 the service had been set up in the Peak District, in Cumbria, London, the West Country and Southern England.

SCOTLAND – CAMPING AND CARAVANNING SITES

The Scottish Tourist Board publishes this guide annually at 70p; add 20p for packing and postage. It is particularly admirable for giving French and German translations of how to find a site, how the licensing system works and how fees are charged. Sites are listed alphabetically, just over thirty symbols are used and there are six pages of maps with site locations. Only those licensed sites that provide a reasonable proportion of pitches for tents are included. This is a well organized little book.

WALES – WHERE TO STAY

This, 75p from bookshops, add 20p for packing and postage, lists details of camp sites in the principality and is similar to the English *Where to Stay* guides. There is also a camping guide at 25p.

NORTHERN IRELAND – CARAVAN AND CAMP SITES

This annual publication issued free of charge by the Northern Ireland Tourist Board, uses thirteen symbols and, whenever possible, quotes costs per night. Another useful publication, *Touring in the Trees,* which lists camp sites in the forests of the six counties, is produced by the Forest Service of the Department of Agriculture and is also free of charge. It includes a booking form and describes the special features of the individual forests.

BRITAIN CAMPING AND CARAVANNING SITES

Published by the British Tourist Authority at £2.25, this covers the whole of England, Scotland, Wales and Northern Ireland. Some of the sites listed are the same as those in the English Tourist Board's books, but this is no means a duplication; the two bodies work independently, the Tourist Authority's chief aim being to promote Britain to overseas visitors. The information in the guide is in five European languages, but the background on sites, which have to conform to minimum Tourist Board standards, should be helpful to English campers. Amusing line drawings break up the text, and, as well as clear directional instructions, there are twenty-four pages of site location maps.

TRAX

This joint Sealink-British Tourist Authority publication offers a number of pitches on racecourse sites, (twenty-three out of ninety-two entries) hence its name. Trax, which costs £1.50, either direct post free from the address given on page 87 or from any of the twenty-three racecourse sites, pays for itself as it contains fourteen 30p vouchers. These can be used at various sites partially to offset the cost of a night's stay. The advantages of camps on race courses are that they are usually close to main roads, they have common rooms with television sets and, because they do not accept reservations, can often offer a pitch when other camps are full.

THE FORESTRY COMMISSION

This organization has around thirty sites open to campers and caravanners in some of the finest parts of the country. The sites, which include thirteen in the New Forest, are graded A and B. Class A sites have flush lavatories and usually a shop and are under the supervision of a full-time warden. Class B sites have minimum facilities and are more suited to caravanners who have their own toilet facilities. Most sites are open from Easter to September, but some remain open throughout the year, offering reduced rates in the low season. There is no advance booking. The main leaflet is available from the Scottish headquarters and a separate one for the New Forest from the Hampshire office (see page 87).

Ireland – Approved Caravan and Camping Parks

An Irish Tourist Board publication costing 50p, this clearly laid out booklet gives full site details, prices, a site location map and details of tent and equipment hire companies.

The National Trust
This charitable organization runs some seventy camp sites on Trust property in England, Wales and Northern Ireland. Send stamped addressed envelope for sheet listing sites and charges.

Camp-site guides: the continent
The four guides to continental camp sites generally available from British bookshops, as well as the leaflets or books on the subject obtainable from the relevant tourist offices, are very similar in layout to English camp-site guides; many of the symbols used will be familiar to English campers. Because European countries use different methods of classification and some use none at all, a number of the European site guides published in England steer clear of any form of classification. The guides are discussed on the following pages, and there is a separate section on guides dealing purely with France, Europe's most popular camping country.

CAMPING AND CARAVANNING IN EUROPE
The AA offers this guide at £3.95; it is published in April. It lists sites in sixteen major European countries and some small ones such as Andorra and Liechtenstein. Information is provided on around four thousand sites, but no classification is given. There are seventy pages of maps showing site locations and major roads.

THE RAC GUIDE TO BRITISH AND CONTINENTAL
CAMPING AND CARAVANNING SITES
New in 1981 and selling at £6.00 this 368-page guide, which includes an excellent 64-page colour atlas showing site locations, gives details of some 5,600 sites in thirty-one countries. The guide provides official and unofficial ratings for the site listed, as well as fifty items of information about each. As there are no descriptions whatsoever of the sites, apart from the symbols and ratings, this guide appears daunting, though it is very efficient. The RAC also produces a number of slim booklets listing sites in individual countries. These, mainly paperbacks, start at around 25p each.

CONTINENTAL CAMPING AND CARAVAN SITES
Produced by *Camping* magazine at £1.55, this lists sites in sixteen European countries. Only eight items of information are given for each site, and this, say the publishers, is because a large number of sites has been included in the book, which is aimed at the touring camper rather than the 'static' holidaymaker. The small maps of each country do not indicate camp-site positions, and apart from the address of the site no directions for how to reach the camps are given under the individual listings. The book has descriptions of

each country, some background information on camping, and vocabulary lists in English, French, German and Spanish.

SELECTED SITES FOR CARAVANNING AND CAMPING IN EUROPE

This guide, by Alan Rogers, costs £1.70 and is published by Deneway Guides. It is similar to his English guide in that it is based on personal experience of the sites. Mr Rogers has visited camps in France, Germany, Italy, Belgium, Austria, Switzerland, Italy, Luxembourg, Liechtenstein, the Netherlands, Spain and Portugal. His personal comments make good reading and are very helpful in painting a picture of a site. Being a camper himself, Mr Rogers knows the importance of site-location maps and includes five in his guide, together with precise instructions of how to get to sites. He also mentions reservations, including details whenever possible, of what system individual sites use.

Camp-site guides: France

CAMPING CARAVANNING FRANCE

This Michelin Guide, at £3.25, is the acknowledged leader of the pack and is published annually in March. Outstanding for its content as well as its shape and colour, which make all the Michelin guides so easily recognizable, the camping guide has been going for twenty-seven years. It gives precise detailed information on over 3,200 French sites, and although the actual text is written in French the explanatory notes, given in four languages, make interpretation easy. The guide has its own 'peak' system of classification which is quite different from the star system used by the French government and should not be confused with it. Sites are listed alphabetically under the name of the nearest town or village, and there are twenty pages of excellent site-location maps with the map number of the relevant Michelin sheet map next to each site. Where necessary, small area maps are included in the text.

WHERE TO CAMP IN FRANCE

Produced by the Camping and Caravanning Club, this guide is published by the Kate Spencer Agency and costs £2.50 from specialist shops or direct from the publishers, post free. Over 800 of France's top sites are listed in the book, every area of the country is covered and every site checked by inspectors who look at cleanliness as well as amenities.

The guide is arranged in regions with sites listed alphabetically under towns. Amenities are listed by symbols and a brief assessment of the site is made.

CAMP SITES IN FRANCE

Published by Letts at £2.50, this guide uses the French government's grading system of stars to denote facilities, and includes an explanation of what the star ratings mean. Almost 5,000 sites are listed alphabetically, grouped region by region under key towns. There is a brief description of each of the twenty regions, which include Corsica, and a site-location map of each. The book is written in English, which might be a comfort to those who do not trust their French. There is a sample booking form at the back of the book.

FRENCH FEDERATION CAMP-SITE GUIDE

This guide is not generally available from bookshops but is well worth sending away for (address page 87, £3.95 including postage) if you want a comprehensive guide to French sites. It lists over 7,000 one- to four-star sites and over 2,000 farm sites. There is a site location map and a list of sites open in the winter. The book is written in French, but there is an English key to the symbols. The 1983 edition comes out in March.

CASTELS & CAMPING CARAVANNING

This leaflet lists some three dozen sites in the grounds of historic houses. The chain, which has a sister organization in Holland, was started in 1959 as a means of helping towards the upkeep of certain old estates and allowing campers to enjoy holidays in unusual settings. The leaflet, called *Castels & Camping Caravanning*, is obtainable from the French office (address on page 85) or from the French Government Tourist Office (address on page 88). Send an A4-size SAE.

European tourist offices

For holidaymakers most tourist offices (addresses on page 88), will provide information on their country ranging from historic background to fact sheets on currency, traffic regulations, shop and bank opening times, what to buy, where to eat, what to see, and so on. The countries where camping is popular can also provide information on camp sites. This varies from single sheets to thick camp-site guides published either by the official camping organization or by the country's leading motoring club. Some countries send all information out free; others, particularly if a heavy book is included, make a charge for what they provide. The following countries, listed alphabetically, provide camping information: remember to write early if you want lists and brochures to arrive before you go on holiday.

AUSTRIA

The government publication *Camping – Caravanning* is issued free by the London tourist office. This excellent detailed annual guide, which includes a site-location map, uses twenty-one symbols to classify sites. Two other useful publications are also free: the general brochure *Austria*, which provides background information on the country, and a big folding map which contains motoring details and thumbnail sketches of the main cities.

BELGIUM

The well run tourist office in London, as well as those in Belgian towns, have a leaflet giving details of more than five hundred licensed camp sites. The sites, which are given star ratings and explanations by symbols, are listed alphabetically, province by province. The list, which does not include sites not officially approved, is free. The publication *Belgium – where to go, what to see*, also free, provides good background information.

DENMARK

The Danish tourist office has a free booklet listing all the two- and three-star sites in the country – some five hundred of them. The Danish Camping Union in Copenhagen (Det Danske Lejrpladsudvalg) publishes an annual handbook which lists all approved sites, while the FDM, the Danish motoring club (Forenede Danske Motorejere), runs twenty-six sites for its own members which may be used by members of sister motoring organizations. Best to wait to buy the camping union's book when you get to Denmark, but a list of the FDM sites can be obtained from its Copenhagen office (address on page 88).

Also helpful are the ninety-six-page booklet *Denmark – land of the welcoming heart*, which provides comprehensive background from historic facts to information on shopping, eating out and so on, and *Denmark for your 1983 holiday*, which gives details of where such activities as golf, fishing and riding can be enjoyed as well as information on half-day courses in spinning, weaving or dying – campers need to find something to do if the weather turns gloomy.

FINLAND

The annual publication of the free booklet *Finland camping* lists 350 sites graded on a one- to three-star basis. Sites tend to be on the coast or near rivers and lakes. The booklet also gives general information on camping in Finland.

FRANCE

The French government tourist office produces an annual guide, around January. It is intended for all holidaymakers and includes addresses of companies which offer rent-a-tent and caravan holidays.

There is plenty of background information on France and a fascinating section on short courses and unusual breaks – many campers may want to go back to do a Cordon Bleu cookery course or to brush up on their French in the Mediterranean. The book is free, but 50p is required to cover postage and packing. The tourist office also issues the *Logis de France,* a guide to over 4,000 small and medium-sized family hotels which make ideal one-night stops for campers on the long trail south. Once again, the publication is free, but packing and postage are 50p. During the summer the tourist office is so busy it cannot accept incoming telephone calls, so write early.

GERMANY

The tourist office for the Federal Republic of Germany (West Germany) issues an annual leaflet giving details of some four hundred of the 2,000 or so sites in the country. The sites included in the leaflet are said to be 'well to excellently equipped', and they are open from May until September with a number, mainly in the winter sports areas, staying open all year. The leaflet, which includes a site-location map, uses the same classification system as the German Camping Club which produces its own guide, as does the German motoring organization, the ADAC (Allgemeiner Deutscher Automobil Club). According to *Happy Days in Germany*, an annual publication which is packed with information, maps and colour pictures, there is no advance booking for German sites. Some camp-site guides however recommend booking. Best is to try, sending an international reply coupon, and see if you get in.

The German Camping Club, the DCC (Deutscher Camping Club), lists some sixteen hundred sites while the ADAC's comprehensive two-volume publication covers most of Europe. If you are interested in either of these guides, it might be easier to buy them in a bookshop when you arrive in Germany than to attempt to order them by post from home. The tourist office in London is not able to supply either of the books. You can, however, get a map of Germany from the tourist office as well as an annually updated leaflet listing all the events taking place from April to October. There is no charge for sending out information.

GREECE

The Greek tourist office can supply lists of sites, about ten pages long, giving names, addresses and sizes of camps, but no maps or directions. There is also an absolutely stunning book *Greece*, full of superb pictures, but with a short information section in French at the back. There is no charge for sending out information.

IRELAND

The Irish tourist office produces excellent material for the holiday-maker. There are free information sheets, numbered 1-56, covering such subjects as seaside resorts, eighteenth-century Dublin, houses, castles and gardens and free attractions. The annual *Caravan and*

Camping Parks costs 50p and is well produced in four languages. There are thorough site descriptions, a clear definition of the four categories of site, and a useful list of companies which hire out camping equipment. *Ireland – Traveller's Guide*, free, is packed with practical information. In 1982 the Irish Tourist Board produced a free leaflet *Special Value Food Fare* aimed at helping the budget-conscious holidaymaker get value for money. It lists hotels and restaurants which provide fixed price menus.

ITALY

The tourist office can supply a map of camp sites free of charge. It is called *Carta Schematica Parchi di Campeggio*. However, the comprehensive guide *Campeggi e Villaggi Turistici in Italia*, produced by the Touring Club Italiano is available only in Italy and costs around 6,000 lire, either from the Club's headquarters in Milan (address page 88) or from bookshops. The guide lists some 3,000 sites in Italy's sixteen regions, and there is an English explanation of the eighty or so symbols used. The tourist office has, free of charge, an excellent publication, *Italy – Traveller's Handbook*. This is packed with useful information about climate, festivals, sport, museums, art galleries and so on.

LUXEMBOURG

The grand duchy of Luxembourg has only 120 camp sites. The tourist office has a free folder listing them all. Also free is the brochure, *Grand Duchy of Luxembourg* which is full of useful information on climate, places of interest, restaurants, the availability of sporting facilities and so on.

THE NETHERLANDS

There are two free publications put out by the national tourist office, *Holland – Camping 1983* and *Camping in Holland*. The first lists 350 of Holland's 2,000 camp sites, which have been selected with the co-operation of the Netherlands Camping Council. The sites have been judged on the quality of their facilities and the space they provide. The second booklet, produced by the CRC (Camping Reserving Centrale), lists sites that can be booked in advance and gives detailed information about the booking service. The organization appears to be most efficient, and there is a reservation form at the end of the book. Another brochure which gives background information is *Holland – General Information*. There is also available a folding sheet map of the country with town plans and information useful to the motorist. The Netherlands has a good tourist structure, and many of the tourist offices, distinguished by the VVV sign (Vereniging voor Vreendelingen Verkeer, which means 'organization for strangers'), will have up-to-date information on local camp sites.

NORWAY

There are over 1,300 classified sites in Norway ranging from one- to three-star standard, the last being very well appointed. The annual camp-site leaflet issued by the Norwegian travel association and available from the national tourist office, lists sites according to their position along the major road system. Ask also for *Affordable Noarway* which gives details of the country's six regions as well as background on camping and information on camp-site chalets.

PORTUGAL

There are only seventy-five camp sites in Portugal, mainly round the coast, although I have heard that not many are actually very close to the beach. A free sheet listing all the sites is available from the national tourist office.

SPAIN

The free sheet *Mapa de Campings España, 1982* lists the camp sites of Spain province by province, using symbols to denote luxury, first-, second- and third-category sites. The site-location map, which also includes main roads and motorways, is very clear and there is a useful chart listing distances (in kilometres) between the capitals of each province. The booklet *Spain* is good for practical, cultural, historic and sporting background, while *Nature in Spain* gives an excellent description of the country's nine national parks. These spectacularly beautiful and enormously varied parks show a face of Spain entirely unknown to those who visit only the coastal regions. All these publications are free. There is also a camp-site guide, *Guida de Campings*, published by the Ministry of Tourism, which can be bought only in Spain; it costs around 200 pesetas.

SWITZERLAND

The national tourist office offers a folding camp-site map, free of charge, which is also an excellent map of Switzerland. It lists 330 of the country's 450 sites, but confusingly the grading system on this map works in reverse order to that of most of the other countries, with three-star sites providing the simplest facilities. The tourist office has two camping books for sale, both annual publications. The guide of the Federation of Swiss Campings costs £2.00, and the guide of the Swiss Camping Association £1.00. There is no charge for packing and postage. Winter sites are listed on a separate sheet. For factual background information obtain *Travel tips for Switzerland* and for general information the wallchart *Switzerland*. This has a gigantic and stunning picture on one side, which can be hung in a child's room after the holiday. The reverse side lists historic, geographic and scientific facts about the country.

SWEDEN

There are two publications worth getting hold of: *Sweden the Natural Choice for your Holiday*, which includes some information on camping, and *Camping Sweden*, an eight-page black and white newspaper-style publication giving plenty of background information as well as a list of camp sites and addresses of companies who run camping packages to Sweden. Once you arrive in Sweden you can obtain the official guide, *Camping platser i Sverigi*, from most bookshops and some of the larger sites. This book, known colloquially as the *Campingbroken*, lists the 561 official sites in Sweden. There is an English explanation for the seventy or so symbols used, and details of the ten simply equipped sites in Sweden where overnight stops are free of charge. The book has an excellent road map showing exact site locations, and costs the equivalent of between £3–£4.

YUGOSLAVIA

The national tourist office has a comprehensive guide to camp sites, well documented and free. The majority of camps are in forests, mountain areas, near lakes or rivers or at the seaside. Ask for three other publications: *Yugoslavia – Travel information, Yugoslavia* and *Yugoslavia – tourist map*. As well as showing the road system, the map also gives distances between towns and background information for drivers.

Addresses

Camp Resa,
123 Rue de l'Université,
75007,
Paris, France.

Camping en Ferme d'Accueil,
BP 901,
Route de Moyrazès,
12009,
Rodex Cedex,
France.

McCarta Ltd,
122 Kings Cross Road,
London WC1.

Campexel,
123 Rue de l'Université,
75007,
Paris, France.

The Camping and Caravanning Club,
11 Lower Grosvenor Place,
London SW1W 0EY.

Castels & Camping Caravanning,
Madame Quida,
9 rue Men Allen,
56470 La Trinité-sur-Mer,
France.

The English Regional Tourist Boards

Cumbria Tourist Board,
Ashleigh,
Holly Road,
Windermere,
Cumbria.
Tel. 096 62 4444

(Cumbria)

East Anglia Tourist Board,
14 Museum Street,
Ipswich,
Suffolk 1P1 1HU.
Tel. 0473 214211

(Norfolk, Suffolk, Essex and Cambridgeshire)

East Midlands Tourist Board
Exchequergate,
Lincoln LN2 1PZ.
Tel. 0522 31521

(Derbyshire, Leicestershire, Lincolnshire, Northampton-shire and Nottinghamshire)

Heart of England Tourist Board,
PO Box 15,
Worcester WR1 2EW.
Tel. 0905 29511

(Gloucestershire, Hereford and Worcester, Shropshire, Staffordshire, Warwickshire and West Midlands)

London Tourist Board,
26 Grosvenor Gardens,
London SW1W 0DU.
Tel. 01-730 3450

(the Greater London area)

Northumbria Tourist Board,
8 Osborne Terrace,
Jesmond,
Newcastle-upon-Tyne NE2 1NT.
Tel. 0632 817744

(Cleveland, Durham, Northumberland, Tyne and Wear)

North-West Tourist Board,
The Last Drop Village,
Bromley Cross,
Bolton,
Lancs BL7 9PZ.
Tel. 0204 591511

(Cheshire, Greater Manchester, Lancashire, Merseyside and the High Peak District of Derbyshire)

South-East England Tourist Board,
Cheviot House,
4-6 Monson Road,
Tunbridge Wells,
Kent TN1 1NH.
Tel. 0892 40766

(East Sussex, Kent, Surrey, West Sussex)

Southern Tourist Board,
The Old Town Hall,
Leigh Road,
Eastleigh,
Hants SO5 4DE.
Tel. 0703 616027

(Hampshire, Eastern Dorset and the Isle of Wight)

Thames and Chilterns Tourist Board
8 The Market Place,
Abingdon,
Oxon OX14 3HG.
Tel. 0235 22711

(Oxfordshire, Berkshire, Bedfordshire, Buckingham-shire and Hertfordshire)

West Country Tourist Board,
Trinity Court,
37 Southernhay East,
Exeter EX1 1QS.
Tel. 0392 76351

(Avon, Cornwall, Devon, Western Dorset, Somerset, Wiltshire, the Isles of Scilly)

Yorkshire and Humberside Tourist Board,
312 Tadcaster Road,
York YO2 2HF.
Tel. 0904 707961

(Humberside, North Yorkshire, West Yorkshire, South Yorkshire)

Other tourist boards in Britain

The English Tourist Board,
4 Grosvenor Gardens,
London SW1W 0DU.

The Scottish Tourist Board,
23 Ravelston Terrace,
Edinburgh EH4 3EU.
Tel. 031 332 2433

The Wales Tourist Board,
Brunel House,
2 Fitzalan Road,
Cardiff CF2 1UY.
Tel. 0222 499909

Northern Ireland Tourist Board,
River House,
48 High Street,
Belfast BT1 2DS.
Tel. 0232 31221

North of Ireland Dept. of Agriculture,
Room 142A,
Dundonald House,
Belfast BTA 3SB.

The Isle of Man Tourist Board,
13 Victoria Street,
Douglas,
Isle of Man,
Tel. 0624 4323

States of Jersey Tourism Committee,
Weighbridge,
St Helier,
Jersey, CI.
Tel. 0534 7800

States of Guernsey Tourism Committee,
PO Box 23,
States Office,
St Peter Port,
Guernsey CI.
Tel. 0481 24411

British Tourist Authority,
239 Old Marylebone Road,
London NW1 5QT.

Other addresses in Britain

Trax,
345 Upper Richmond Road,
London SW15 6XP.

The Forestry Commission,
231 Corstorphine Road,
Edinburgh EH12 7AT.

For details of New Forest sites write to:

The Forestry Commission,
Seaman's Lodge,
Minstead,
Lyndhurst,
Hants SO4 7FU.

The National Trust,
42 Queen Annes Gate,
London SW1H 9AS.

French Federation Campsite Guide,
6 The Meadows,
Worlington,
Bury St Edmunds,
Suffolk 1P28 8SH.

The Kate Spencer Agency
26 Commercial Buildings,
Dunston,
Gateshead NE11 9AA.

European tourist offices

Austrian National Tourist Office,
30 St George Street,
London W1R 9FA.

Belgian National Tourist Office,
38 Dover Street,
London W1X 3RB.

The Danish Tourist Board,
Sceptre House,
169/173 Regent Street,
London W1R 8PY.

The Danish Camping Union,
Skjoldgade 10,
2100 Copenhagen Ø,
Denmark.

FDM Camping,
Blegdamsvej 124,
2100 Copenhagen Ø,
Denmark.

Finnish Tourist Board,
66-68 Haymarket,
London SW1Y 4RF.

French Government Tourist Office,
178 Piccadilly,
London W1V 0AL.

German National Tourist Office,
61 Conduit Street,
London W1R 0EN.

National Tourist Organization of Greece,
195-197 Regent Street,
London W1R 8DL.

Irish Tourist Board,
Ireland House,
158 New Bond Street,
London W1Y 0AQ.

Italian State Tourist Office,
201 Regent Street,
London W1R 8AY.

Touring Club of Italy
Corso Italia, 10,
Milan,
Italy.

Luxembourg National Tourist Office,
36-37 Piccadilly,
London W1V 9PA.

Netherlands National Tourist Office,
Savory & Moore House,
143 New Bond Street,
London W1Y 9FD.

Norwegian National Tourist Office,
20 Pall Mall,
London SW1.

Portuguese National Tourist Office,
New Bond Street House,
1/5 New Bond Street,
London W1Y 0NP.

Spanish National Tourist Office,
57/58 St James's Street,
London SW1A 1LD.

Swedish National Tourist Office,
3 Cork Street,
London W1X 1HA.

Swiss National Tourist Office,
Swiss Centre,
1 New Coventry Street,
London W1V 3HG.

Yugoslav National Tourist Office,
143 Regent Street,
London W1R 8AE.

Examples of letters for booking a pitch on a camp site

English
Remember to include a stamped and self-addressed envelope for reply.
Dear Sir,

I would like to stay at your site for .... days. Arriving on .... and leaving on ....
There are .... people in my party, ... adults and .... children, aged .... We will need a pitch for our tent and parking space for a car.

Would you please send me a list of your charges and the amount of deposit you require.

For continental bookings remember to send an international reply coupon and your own name and address.

French
Monsieur,

*Je me propose de séjourner à votre terrain de camping pour ....
jours depuis le .... jusq'au ....*
Nous sommes .... personnes en tout, y compris .... adultes et .... enfants, âgés de .... Nous aurons besoin d'un emplacement pour notre tente et notre voiture.

Veuillez me donner dans votre réponse votre tarif de prix en m'indiquant en même temps le montant que vous demandez comme arrhes.

German
Sehr geehrter Herr,

Ich beabsichtige mich auf ihrem Campingplatz .... Tage aufzuhalten und zwar vom¯.................... bis zum ....
Wir sind im ganzen .... Personen .... Erwachsene und .... Kinder im Alter von .... und benötigen Platz für Zelt und unseren Wagen.

Bitte geben Sie mir in ihrem Antwortschreiben die vollen Preise bekannt und ebenso die Höhe der von mir zu leistenden Anzahlung.

Italian

Egregio Signore,

Ho intenzione di rimanere presso di voi per .... giorni arriverò il .... e partirò il ....
Siamo un gruppo di .... adulti e .... bambini, di età ....
Vorremmo un posto per tenda e spazio per parcheggiare la nostra vettura.

Vi preghiamo di quotare i prezzi completi quando ci risponderete e di darci informazioni sul deposito richiesto.

Spanish

Muy señor mio,

Desearia me reservara espacio por .... dias a partir del .... hasta el .... Nuestro grupo se compañe de .... adultos y .... niños de .... años de edad. Necesitaremos un espacio por tienda y espacio para aparcar.

Le ruego nos comunique los precios y nos informe sobre el depósito.

4
Preparation and Getting There

The rent-a-tent companies, just like the tour operators, issue their brochures annually, often before Christmas. By early spring therefore, prudent campers planning to take a rent-a-tent package, particularly those restricted to the school holidays, will have made their bookings and so will have little to do until it is time to obtain their foreign currency, check their documentation and depart.

Families using their own gear will have a great deal more work to do in the months before the holiday, however, particularly if they plan to go abroad. Apart from getting all the equipment out of the loft or garage and checking to see what has to be repaired, replaced or abandoned, they will have to face the dreaded task of booking a ferry crossing.

Maintenance and repair of camping equipment

Wait for the first fine day in spring to get the camping equipment out. Ideally, take it all off on a weekend's 'test' camp. This will soon show if the tent is still weatherproof, if the jets have become blocked in the cooker, or if the fabric has rotted on the chairs!

Experts recommend that tents should, if possible, be stored open during the winter. Clearly most campers cannot manage to do this; neither do most of us, as we are told to, get the tent out once or twice during the winter and put it up to air. The majority of us, to be honest, get everything out just before we set off and just hope that it won't fall to pieces when we get to the site.

TENTS

The tent is the most important item. If it has been put away dry and clean, it should still be in good condition when you next want to use it, but if it has been stored either damp or in damp conditions it might have become mildewed. Mildew is a fungus which attacks fabrics that have been stored in wet or damp conditions and if not treated it will rot the canvas. Should there be any signs of mildew, brush it off carefully and, if the fabric is not damaged, clean the tent, mend any tears and re-proof the mildewed area of the canvas. If just a small area is affected, use just a can of aerosol re-proofer; if the whole tent has to be treated, use a brush or a garden spray to put the re-proofing liquid on. Should the mildew stain not just brush off, wipe the affected part of the canvas with a weak solution of Milton. If the stain persists, try a solution of two parts hydrogen peroxide to one part potassium permanganate. Allow the area to dry thoroughly before applying the re-proofing compound.

If the tent is not mildewed but you think it may need re-proofing (this is usually necessary every three or four years), test it by putting it up in the garden, preferably when rain is due – but as a last resort, spray it with a hose. If the water does not soak through, the tent is in good order; if, however, water starts to drip through on the inside, it is time to re-proof.

Incidentally, if you want to have a tent re-proofed but have not the space to do it at home, it can be done commercially. Ask in a camping shop whether they provide this service or look in the yellow pages for a company which will do it; see also the list of addresses on page 117. As with lawn-mower servicing, commercial tent re-proofing should ideally be carried out in the winter rather than just before the holiday. Commercial concerns will also undertake major repairs to tents such as mending damaged storm walls, putting in new zips or making awnings or canopies. More about tent repairs on page 94. Repairs to small tears can, of course, be carried out at home, and should be done before re-proofing. Buy canvas or nylon patches and the appropriate adhesive from a camping shop.

There are various kinds of re-proofing compounds available, so make sure to get the right sort for your tent. At least three companies make re-proofing and Caseys list compounds in their catalogue. Grangersol, whose products are sold in most camping shops, make a wide range of re-proofing and treatment products for tents and camping gear, including airbed repair kits, shampoo for down sleeping bags and lead-free stove fuel. Write for catalogue (address page 118).

It is worth noting that re-proofing compounds are designed for tents that actually need to be treated and they will not 'take' on canvas that is not absorbent, i.e. that does not need to be re-proofed, hence the need to test beforehand. Generally speaking, the more absorbent the fabric the more proofing it will absorb, so bear the age and condition of your tent in mind when calculating how much re-proofer to buy. These days most re-proofing compounds have a silicone base and are easy to use. They are available in cans, bottles or aerosols and are applied by brush, spraygun or straight from an aerosol container. (If a spraygun is used, a cheap garden spray will do, but keep it solely for re-proofing.) Other re-proofers are based on either water or wax emulsion, the wax-based kind taking the longest time to dry. As the tent should not be rained on during this job, try to pick a couple of fine days for re-proofing.

Once you have established that re-proofing is necessary, proceed as follows. Put the tent up, brush it thoroughly and remove any stubborn marks. *Never* use detergent, as this destroys the waterproofing, but use instead a cleaning product specially made for tents; Grangersol produces one. Grease marks can be removed by backing the canvas with blotting paper or absorbent brown paper and rubbing the mark with Fabsil waterproofing. When the tent has been brushed and cleaned and has dried, the re-proofing can start, so lower it to its 'knees' and begin with the roof, using the brush or spray as evenly as possible to avoid patches. Put the tent back to its full height and, always working downwards, re-proof a wall at a time until the job is finished.

Your general inspection of the tent should also naturally include the inner tents. Often the sew-in groundsheet can begin to leak after years of use on gritty ground. To this problem there are two solutions: either buy another groundsheet and just lay it on top of the existing one or, if you like everything really neat, tidy and ship-shape, cut out the old sheet and, using it as a pattern, make a new one. The latter course of action requires a strong sewing machine; otherwise get a tent repairer to do the job. The heavy-duty groundsheets used in the living area of the tent can be patched quite satisfactorily.

Check guy ropes, which can fray, rubbers for signs of perishing, tapes, which tend to get torn off, zips in case sliders have come off and teeth are missing, and tent pegs, which always seem to become lost or bent. Examine the frame of the tent and replace any distorted lengths of tubing. If the spring links used in the frame have become overstretched, it is easy to replace them using a special tool stocked by camp shops; it costs about 50p.

BEDDING

Airbeds, being made from a rubber-based fabric, have a limited life and if, when pumped up, they just go down for no apparent reason, they have become porous and will have to be replaced. This is where campbeds score, for their life seems to be endless: some families hand them down from generation to generation. To prolong their life, airbeds should not be over-inflated and should be stored rolled or flat rather than folded. Blow a little French chalk down the inflation valve occasionally – to help prevent the inside walls of the airbed from sticking together.

Sleeping bags should have been washed or dry-cleaned before being stored, and these should now be aired, and their zips checked and if necessary replaced. When sleeping bags have been dry-cleaned it is most important that they should be aired to get rid of the cleaning fumes, which can be lethal, before they are used or stored away. There are now some special shampoos on the market for cleaning down or feather sleeping bags at home.

COOKING AND LIGHTING EQUIPMENT

Clean the stove thoroughly as dust can get into the jets during storage. Remove the burners and clean them, making sure that you use a proper jet cleaner – camping shops sell special very fine jet pricks for this purpose. Do not attempt to use domestic sewing needles – they are far too thick and will damage the jets. If the cooker is made by a reputable manufacturer, any necessary spare parts should not be difficult to come by. Check that the hose connecting the stove to the gas container is not worn. If you have any doubts, replace the hose – do not try to repair it. Check pressure valves and rubber sealing washers. If you have an old stove, perhaps a high-pressure model, it might be worth considering buying a new one. There have been a number of improvements, especially from the safety angle, over the past few years (see page 30).

Do not forget to examine the picnic stove at the same time. This is just a case of seeing that the rubber sealing washer where the burner unit is attached to the gas cartridge has not perished. Stock up with cartridges for the picnic stove and lanterns. Check that there are spare gas mantles for lanterns and replace damaged lamp glasses, however small the crack or chip.

TABLES AND CHAIRS

If you use chairs with canvas or man-made fibre seats, check that the stitching is sound and that the material has not worn away where it passes behind the metal rod at the back of the seat. Renew the fabric if there is any sign of wear, making sure you buy the correct width. Hardware shops as well as camping stores sell pre-cut lengths of canvas or nylon material. If you have chairs with bar and spring attachments, replacement kits can be obtained from camping shops, larger branches of Woolworths and the House of Holland.

On camping tables with adjustable legs, make sure all the screws are in place. Oil the hinges and screws on both tables and chairs, but not too much, wiping away any surplus oil.

MISCELLANEOUS

Even though crockery and cutlery will have been put away washed and clean, it is worth washing it again for the new season. Cool boxes should be rinsed out with a solution of water and bicarbonate of soda, and water carriers with Milton. Check ice sachets: the soft variety deteriorate after a few years' use and may need to be replaced.

TENT REPAIRS

Finally, if your tent needs any major repair work, check, if it is comparatively new, whether it is still under guarantee and if so take it back to the shop from which you bought it. Bear in mind that only damage resulting from faulty workmanship can be carried out under guarantee. If the tent has been damaged by bad weather, incorrect handling or neglect, the customer will be expected to pay for any work carried out. Even if the tent is out of guarantee it is worth taking it back to the shop it came from: reliable concerns offer a repair service on equipment bought from them.

If you need to find a tent repair company look in the yellow pages; however, as there are not all that many such companies in the country addresses of some reliable organizations are given on page 117. A number of repair companies advertise in the camping magazines.

Most repairers like to see a tent before giving an estimate, so while they are quite happy to accept work sent to them they prefer personal callers. If you have no choice but to send the tent away, check to see whether post, rail or road services provide the most cost effective way of transport, and do include a list of the work to be carried out, stating precisely what has to be done and to which part of the tent or frame. As transport charges are high think twice about sending a tent away for a minor repair job.

Some repair companies specialize: one in repairs to frames, another in heavy-duty zips or patching obsolete canvases. Some companies operate their own collection and delivery service, some even operate a 24-hour emergency service, so write to a number of organizations to find out what is available and what the scale of charges is.

Maps

It is essential to get good maps at the early stages of route planning and working out overnight stops. Small-scale motorist's maps are useful for the journey and large-scale Ordnance Survey, or the local equivalent, for exploring the region when you arrive at the camp site. Most good rent-a-tent companies include a route map in their pack, and some even include a local map of the area which you are visiting. The colouring of a map is most important, particularly when it is to be used for motoring. Dark coloured roads stand out better in poor light than pale ones.

BRITISH MAPS

British cartographers have traditionally excelled in good, clear road maps. Some of those published by the oil companies are particularly helpful: the Shell road maps, for example, sold by garages for about 40p each (not the 'Supermaps' sold in shops) are very easy to use. There are nine in the series, using a scale of approximately 4.8

kilometres (3 miles) to the inch, with just sufficient detail for easy motoring and no distraction of contour lines or background colouring.

Bartholomew, which has been publishing maps for 150 years, has a series of ten GT maps for the British Isles. These, revised about every three years, have a scale of 6.4 kilometres (4 miles) to the inch and again little distracting detail. The same company produces a yearly catalogue which contains the most useful aid any cartographer can produce for the uninitiated – a guide to the completely baffling fraction scale used on most maps.

The AA's motorists' maps, a series of six for the UK, have a scale of 8 kilometres (5 miles) to the inch, and are good and clear as are the four Michelin maps of England, with a scale of 10 kilometres (6.2 miles) to the inch and a key in five languages, including Welsh. The famous large-scale Ordnance Survey maps with their wealth of detail are invaluable for those who want to explore the country around their camp site. They are also helpful to the motorist, particularly on the last leg of a journey to a remote site when there is insufficient detail on a motoring map. Remember that it is often easier to buy these Ordnance Survey maps, particularly of the less popular areas of the country, when you arrive at your destination: small bookshops just cannot stock the whole series – not surprising as it takes 214 of the 3 centimetres (1¼-inch)-to-one-mile maps to cover the country.

EUROPEAN MAPS

Until recently it always seemed better to buy maps of the European country to be visited on arrival, unless they were obtainable from a motoring organization beforehand. Now, however, most good bookshops in this country offer an excellent selection, although large-scale maps of a particular area will probably still have to be bought on arrival or ordered from a map specialist.

Collins, whose road atlas of Britain sells very well, brought out a road atlas of Europe in 1982. This very clear book of 104 pages costing £4.95, includes maps of 85 city centres and illustrations of 120 international road signs. It is the first large-format atlas of Europe on sale in this country and is particularly helpful at the route-planning stage of the holiday.

France seems to have better coverage than other European countries, boasting forty-two splendid Michelin maps (numbers 51 to 93) at a scale of 1 centimetre to 2 kilometres (0.4 inch to 1.2 miles). There are also large-scale maps of certain areas, and the famous Michelin map, number 989 which covers the entire country. Michelin also produces maps for other European countries. Its map of Europe, number 920, with a scale of 1:3,000 000, is helpful for 'initial' route planning.

The Institut Géographique National, which produces fifteen good 1 centimetre-to-2.5 kilometres (0.4 inch to 1.5 miles) tourist maps of France with useful information on festivals, events, museums and so on, launched a new series of maps last year. These, with a scale of 1 centimetre to 1 kilometre (0.4 inch to 0.6 mile), should, like our Ordnance Survey maps, be invaluable to a family with a sense of adventure. Write to the British agents, McCarta Ltd in London (address on page 118) if you cannot get them locally. The Institut also produces excellent motorway maps of Belgium, Germany and Switzerland. McCarta are also sole agents for Mairs and Kompass, publishers of road and walking maps covering the alpine areas of Germany, Austria and Italy.

The famous 'Bison Futé' map ('Cunning Bison'), showing alternative routes through France, is published yearly by the French Ministry of Transport and is available free from early summer onwards. It is obtainable from garages and some tourist offices in France. The French Government Tourist Office in London is not able to supply copies of the map. This 'Bison Futé' map, an ingenious attempt to induce visitors to France to ease the pressure on the popular tourist routes during the high season, has been so popular during the high season that it has been quite difficult to obtain. It is now available in Britain from AA service centres, travel agencies and port offices.

For members unsure of their ability to work out a route of their own, the AA will provide, at a small charge, a map marked up with the route required. A number of route-planning publications are available to members of this organization, including the Overseas Route Planning Series, reissued by popular request. Details of all route publications and what they cost, are listed on a pink fact sheet; from AA offices. Apply for route material at least three weeks before going on holiday.

If you are in London, it is worth calling at the country's largest map specialists, Stanfords of Covent Garden (address on page 118). As well as stocking standard and unusual maps, Stanfords have a good selection of paperbacks on travel.

For those requiring maps in a hurry, the GB Car Club makes a point of speedy mail order. It can supply the latest edition of any map, generally within forty-eight hours of receipt of order. It also provides a 'Courier Kit' which contains a route-planning map of Europe, the relevant Michelin Guide in English, and maps of the area you plan to visit.

Finally, if you intend to spend some part of your holiday

walking, remember that the Fédération Française de la Randonne Pédestre produces guides to the *grandes randonnes* – national footpaths, rather like our Pennine Way or Ridgway Walk. As well as providing maps of suggested routes and the time it takes to walk them (some are as short as 2 kilometres or 1.2 miles), the guides give a running commentary on what to look out for – a beautiful fourteenth-century church, battle sites, places of geographic interest or outstanding natural beauty and, being French, the specialities of restaurants or inns *en route*. Further details of the guides, which are written in simple French, are available from McCarta Ltd. This company, until 1982 IGN Maps (UK) Ltd, has an excellent selection of motoring and leisure maps, including walking maps, for most European countries. As well as running a well stocked shop, the company has a mail order service. The address is on page 118.

Documentation

Whether you are camping independently or with a rent-a-tent company, there are a number of documents you will need, not forgetting your cross Channel ferry tickets. Aim to have all this documentation complete at least two weeks before the holiday. Remember that passports and insurance documents can be slow to arrive in the high season.

PASSPORTS

The first document needed for travelling abroad is a passport. Everyone over the age of sixteen must have one. A full passport, which is valid for ten years, costs £11. Children under sixteen can be included on either of their parents' passports.

Passport forms can be obtained from post offices, some travel agents or from one of the six UK passport offices. Form A is for standard passports, form B is for children under sixteen who need a full passport and form CAF must be completed by adults intending to add any of their children to their own passport. A 'family' passport is issued jointly to a husband and wife at no extra charge. However only the holder of the passport, be it man or wife, may travel alone on the passport, the second signatory may not. Completed forms should be returned to the relevant passport office together with the necessary documentation. Originals are needed: photostat copies of birth or marriage certificates are not accepted. Send also two full-face photographs, one countersigned by a British citizen who has known you for at least two years. The photographs have to conform to a certain size. Allow at least a month for the processing of a passport application.

If you have forgotten to get or renew a passport, if one of your children has turned sixteen and has not yet been issued with one, or if you just need a passport for a short trip, get a visitor's passport. They cost £5.50 each and are issued over the post-office counter. Take along proof of identity as well as the two photographs (they need not be countersigned in this case), your birth certificate and marriage licence (if applicable). A pension book or driving licence will also be accepted as proof of identification if necessary.

VISAS

A visa is not normally required for western European countries when visits are for less than three months. You will, however, need a visa if you are entering Czechoslovakia, East Germany, Hungary, Poland, Romania or the USSR. Apply to the consulate of the country or countries concerned.

DRIVING LICENCE

A full British driving licence is accepted in most European countries. If more than one adult plans to drive, each should take their own licence. If you are going to Spain, Hungary or Poland, you will need an international driving permit. These can be obtained from motoring organizations. The Italians require a driving licence translation, which is obtainable from the AA or RAC for their own members, otherwise the Italian tourist office will provide a free translation. Free translations are also provided by the ACI (Italian Automobile Club) at frontier and provincial offices.

VEHICLE REGISTRATION DOCUMENT

It is easy to forget this document, sometimes known as the log book. If you are involved in an accident you will be asked to produce this document. If you plan to use a hired car you must get a Hired Vehicle Certificate (HVC). The AA can supply these to anyone who applies.

BAIL BOND

A bail bond, a form of insurance, is needed by motorists in Spain. If you are in a motoring accident in Spain the car can be impounded and you can be put in jail unless a deposit is paid to cover liability. The bail bond provides for this eventuality and is proof that your insurance company will pay any claim. The bond is obtainable from your motor insurance company and costs only a couple of pounds.

GREEN-CARD INSURANCE

This international motor insurance document, which is printed on green paper, provides motorists with full cover abroad. Although it is no longer essential in most countries, it is wise to take it to ensure that your car is fully covered. Although UK insurance policies are valid in the EEC and certain other European countries, their cover abroad is not always the same as at home. The green card provides comprehensive cover. It is available from your car insurance company and costs range from £7 to £40, depending on the company, the car and the length of the holiday. Allow at least a month for processing.

GB STICKER

A GB sticker or plate must be attached to the back of your car. It must be oval in shape with black letters on a white background. Stickers are usually provided free of charge by ferry companies or motoring organizations. Dover Harbour Board supply them free to anyone who has forgotten or has not been able to obtain one elsewhere.

CAMPING CARNET

An international camping carnet offers third-party insurance and is a guarantee to site owners that the organization which issued it will pay for any damage done or any unpaid site fees. The carnet is useful in that it is generally accepted as proof of identity in lieu of a passport when booking into a camp site. Camping clubs and motoring organizations issue carnets to members only; the GB Car club has facilities for issuing them to non-members. Carnets cost about £1.00 each. One carnet only is needed per family.

MEDICAL INSURANCE: FORM 111

British travellers in EEC countries can obtain emergency medical treatment on the same basis as the inhabitants of that country. To be able to take advantage of this reciprocal treatment, a member of the family who pays national insurance contributions must fill in form CM1 on the back of the leaflet number SA30, *Medical Treatment During Visits Abroad*, issued by the Department of Health and Social Security and available from your local office. (Also available from the same source is leaflet SA36, *How to get Medical Treatment in the other EEC Countries*, which you should take with you on holiday.) Form 111 will be issued on completion of form CM1 and must be taken abroad with you. You pay for the treatment, get the doctor or dentist to fill in form 111, and then claim the money when you get home.

Incidentally, there are now ten countries in the EEC: Belgium, Denmark, France, West Germany, the Irish Republic, Italy, Luxembourg, the Netherlands, the United Kingdom (but not the Channel Islands) and Greece.

PRIVATE INSURANCE

The reciprocal health agreement of the EEC countries can fall short of all that is needed. It is aimed chiefly at covering the cost of providing emergency help and does not always provide all treatment free of charge. You may, for example, have to face additional hospital charges, which in many continental countries start at around £60 a day. So it is worth taking out some form of private insurance when on holiday, at home or abroad.

Families travelling with rent-a-tent companies should check that insurance is part of their package. Those camping independently must make their own arrangements. Generally, five or six standard areas of cover come under one premium. This makes provision for cancellation, medical expenses, personal accident, loss or damage to baggage and personal belongings and personal liability (i.e., when you damage someone or something). Expect to pay between £8 to £10 per person for this kind of cover for a fortnight's holiday. Some organizations have a reduction for children under fourteen.

You will also need insurance for the car, over and above that provided by the green card, to cover breakdowns and, if the worst happens and the car becomes unusable, either provide another car for the journey or get the family home. Both the AA and the RAC put insurance packages together for motorists going abroad, and the AA's five-star service is available to non-members. Alternatively, you could obtain quotes from a local agent. If you need help in finding a local broker, contact the British Insurance Brokers Association which can provide a list of members in various parts of the country. If you have any complaints about insurance, get in touch with the consumer information department of the British Insurance Association. (The address is on page 119.)

The AA reckons that the average family camping abroad independently spends about £50 on total insurance, a reasonable investment when it is considered that the majority of claims paid out are for amounts round the £150 to £250 mark.

Campers who have expensive equipment, for example, cine cameras, boats or fishing gear, should find out about extra cover for these items. Those owning their own camping equipment should think about year-round insurance for their gear, especially if they take weekend breaks as well as an annual holiday. Fennel, Turner and Taylor, as well as Europa Insurance, specialize in this type of cover. Europ Assistance offers an overall breakdown protection plan which includes the cost of hiring a replacement tent if yours is damaged accidentally. West Mercia insurance brokers have been specializing in insuring walkers, skiers, climbers and back-packers for the past thirteen years. The company, which recently widened its scope to include family campers, offers a policy that gives cover against loss or damage to camping equipment when it is in use and when it is stored at home.

Finally, do remember that if you are involved in a motoring accident you should inform your insurance company by letter within 24 hours. When luggage or personal effects are missing, make a claim within seven days. Do read the small print before setting off on holiday: you will then be better equipped to deal with an emergency should one arise.

Ordering foreign currency

Order foreign currency a month or so before going on holiday to allow for unexpected delays. Hanging on till the last minute waiting for the change in the rate of exchange to work in your favour never yields much profit and can of course work against you. Last year P&O Ferries introduced a 48-hour complete foreign currency service to people travelling on its ferries. Payments can be made by cheque, postal order or cash, and the commission charged is 1½ percent with a minimum charge of 75p per transaction.

TRAVELLER'S CHEQUES

In spite of the almost universal acceptance of many credit cards abroad, most people still like to take the bulk of their holiday money in traveller's cheques, either in sterling or in the currency of the country to be visited. Until recently most people obtained these cheques from their bank or in some cases through a travel agent, but more outlets are becoming available. As well as the service offered by P&O a number of building societies have now started issuing traveller's cheques to customers. This is a particularly useful service as many building societies are open on Saturday mornings.

Traveller's cheques have to be signed in the bank or place of issue by the person who ordered them and then again in the bank where they are to be cashed. It makes sense, therefore, for each adult to have some in their own name. It can be restricting when one adult controls all the cash. Do not take cheques for very small amounts – never less than £10 or you will spend all your time running to the bank.

A sensible course of action is to take half your cheques in sterling and half in the currency of the country you are visiting and use the sterling ones last. Sterling cheques last indefinitely and can be kept at home until the next visit abroad, whereas a charge will be made after a holiday when traveller's cheques drawn on another country are re-banked. As to which is the cheaper form of cheque to buy depends very much on currency fluctuations and on how many countries you plan to visit. Home banks charge for sterling traveller's cheques; some charge 1 percent while others have a minimum issuing charge of £2. There will then be an added charge for cheques for another country. On these foreign cheques the rate of exchange may work in your favour or it may not. However, if you plan to camp in two or more countries and think it may be cheaper to take sterling cheques and pay only one lot of commission, remember that, while you will pay only one commission in this country, you will have to pay commission in each country where you cash sterling cheques.

Try to cash cheques at banks. Although exchanges (rather like money shops), hotels, some restaurants and shops will exchange cheques they can charge more commission than banks. Remember that you will need proof of identity when cashing traveller's cheques, usually a passport.

Many of the big European camp sites have a mobile bank calling once or twice a week. Days and times will be given on the camp notice board in the reception area.

Most banks that issue traveller's cheques operate a refund service in the case of loss or theft. You should be given details of this service when the cheques are issued to you. Most of the major banks have authorised agents abroad who can make immediate refunds of up to £150 as long as certain conditions are complied with.

Finally, when ordering traveller's cheques and foreign currency ask if any restrictions apply to the currency you are buying. Some countries do not allow bank notes of certain denominations to leave their country; others prohibit the export of all bank notes.

CASH

When ordering traveller's cheques ask for some cash in the currency of the country you are visiting too. You will probably need some as soon as you arrive for motorway tolls, buying food or paying for a night's accommodation. Coins are useful for parking meters and for 'quality' public lavatories.

BANK CARDS

Bank cards can now be used in forty European countries in the same way as in England, to draw money from a bank. Look for a bank displaying the Eurocheque symbol, a large blue E and a red C. Single cheques up to £50 can be drawn on a personal account. Only one encashment a day is permitted and this must not exceed a total of £100, i.e. two cheques of £50 each. Do not forget to take your cheque book as well as your bank card. In an effort to halt international cheque frauds the major British banks are planning to prohibit the use of bank cards overseas. By spring of 1983 travellers may be asked to use Eurocheque cards. Generally speaking, banks recommend that you use your cheque book abroad for emergencies only, because the foreign bank will make a negotiating charge for a sterling cheque.

CREDIT CARDS

Credit cards, chiefly Barclaycard (Visa), Access and Trustcard are now widely accepted abroad and provide an excellent way of buying a number of goods, particularly petrol: it is far nicer to spend the holiday cash feeding the family rather than the car!

CHARGE CARDS

The difference between a credit card and a charge or debit card is that with a credit card you pay, if you wish, only a certain amount of the debt each month, whereas with a charge card you have to pay the whole bill at the end of the month. The advantage of these cards is that there is usually no defined spending limit. Credit cards are issued free, but you have to pay to get a charge card. The American Express and Diner's Club charge cards are widely accepted in Europe.

There are a number of advantages to using bank, credit or charge cards abroad: you are not charged any currency commission, the rate at which sterling is converted into foreign currency is more favourable than that available at banks and bureaux de change, you do not have to settle your bills for several weeks (it can sometimes take months for European bills to filter through) and, finally, you may find it easier to hire a car or pay certain bills if you can produce such a card.

NATIONAL GIROBANK

The National Girobank has become involved in foreign currency dealings. Holders of a Girobank guarantee card can obtain postcheques which enable them to draw local currency up to the value of £50 at any one time at over eighty thousand foreign post offices. There is no commission charged when the transaction is made, but a 50p charge is levied when the cheque returns to England. The good point about the Girobank system is that post offices are often open when banks are closed. Thomas Cook's have a special arrangement with the National Girobank for the issuing of traveller's cheques; ask at a Cook's travel agency.

VISA

A European refund referral service was introduced some years ago for holders of Visa traveller's cheques. Anyone losing these cheques in Europe can make a free call to Visa's European centre which is then routed to London at no charge to the caller. For the initial contact, the switchboard, manned 24 hours a day, 365 days a year, is staffed by multi-lingual operators, so there is no language difficulty. It is on occasions such as this that it is important to have a record of the serial numbers of the lost cheques. You will also need the name of the bank from which you bought the cheques and the date of purchase. Once your identity has been established you will be given the name of the nearest bank from where you can claim your refund. There are over 15,000 member banks in the scheme, including practically every one in France. In total there are more than 35,000 bank branches around the world. This means that you should be able to get replacement cheques at or near your holiday destination. Visa traveller's cheques can be obtained in this country from Barclays Bank, the Bank of Scotland and all branches of the Trustee Savings Banks.

Finally, make a note of the serial numbers of traveller's cheques and the numbers of your credit card, bank card, bank account number and passport. Keep this list in a separate place from the items to which it refers so that if your handbag or wallet is lost or stolen you have a record of what is missing.

Getting the car ready

Make sure the car has a major service before the holiday, particularly if it is to be taken abroad, and do not forget to check the condition of the tyres. Once the vehicle is in good running order, there are certain jobs that have to be done if you plan to drive on the continent. Left-dipping headlights are not allowed in right-hand drive countries, so you will have to get an adaptor set, available from most car accessory shops. Be sure to get the right kit for your model of car as there are a number of different types on sale. If you plan to do any night driving in France you will need yellow headlights. Either paint the outside of the headlamp glass with a removable yellow plastic paint or buy an amber lens convertor kit. Do not forget to re-adjust the headlights to left-hand dip when the holiday is over.

It is well worth fitting an outside mirror on the passenger side of the car if there is not one there already. Passengers in British cars driving on the continent have an active role to play, particularly when you are overtaking. An extra safety precaution is a second inside mirror to help the passengers check the road behind before the driver pulls out to overtake.

A warning triangle is compulsory when driving almost anywhere on the continent. This should have a reflective finish so that it can be used at night as well as during the day.

An emergency windscreen is not compulsory anywhere but is useful, particularly in bad weather, as it can be dangerous driving in heavy rain with a shattered windscreen. The good-quality plastic screens, weatherproofed and steel-reinforced, can be fitted quite easily and allow both windscreen wipers and washers to be used.

If you do not intend to travel often in Europe you might consider hiring an emergency kit instead of going to the expense of making up your own. The AA offers a box of useful spares – fan belt, plugs, points, headlamp bulb, fuses, and so on. The hire charge is around 50p a day but a deposit of £20 is needed. Emergency windscreens and warning triangles can be hired separately. Returnable deposits start at £10.

Whether you holiday in Europe or England it is always worth carrying a tow rope. The best are made specially for the purpose with loops or quick-release devices at each end. It is also useful to keep an old rug in the car for lying on when changing tyres or inspecting the underside of the car.

Finally, it gives a good psychological boost at the start of a holiday to begin the journey in a clean car. To keep the car reasonably tidy on the journey, either invest in a special waste bin that fits across the transmission or keep a plastic bag in the back for all those apple cores and toffee papers. More specific information on driving in Europe is given in Chapter 6.

Booking a ferry

Years ago, when continental travel was not so popular, crossing the Channel was reasonably simple because there was not much choice available in the way of ferry services. Now, with well over twenty million passengers making the crossing each year, most of them during the summer months, and with an armada of ships available to ferry them to a choice of twenty-two ports in eight continental countries, the problem of what ferry to book and from and to which port can be confusing: there are just too many choices available. The best course of action in this situation is to eliminate any unnecessary information right at the start – do not attempt to read every single ferry brochure. Some effective pruning can be done by studying two good road maps, one of England and the other showing the European coastline and the country in which you intend to travel. Then, taking into consideration where you live and where you plan to holiday, work out which port is best for departure from England and which for arrival on the continent.

The fact that Dover is the busiest port in the UK, used by over twelve and a half million passengers and over one and a half million cars a year, does not necessarily mean that it is the best exit for everyone. There are twenty ports round the English coast serving terminals in Scandinavia, Holland, Germany, France, Spain and Ireland. Doing your homework carefully can save time, money and frustration when it comes to setting off on holiday. Five factors should be taken into consideration when booking a ferry: the amount of driving to be done, both here and on the continent; the cost of petrol; the cost and the length of the crossing; and the possibility of making overnight stops, either in this country or fairly soon after crossing the Channel. Sometimes taking a cabin for an overnight crossing can be a better proposition than an overnight stay in a hotel or camp site on the continent or in this country before leaving on a very early crossing. However, check what time the boat arrives and, if it is in the small hours, find out whether you are allowed to stay on board until a reasonable hour in the morning – being deposited in Calais at 0200 hours with a couple of cross children does not make the best start to a holiday. Staying on board is generally allowed on the longer sea crossings only.

If western France or Brittany is the holiday destination, a crossing to Le Havre, Cherbourg or St Malo could be your best bet, assuming that you want to avoid that rather tedious drive through northern France. Your final destination will, however, depend on where you live in the United Kingdom.

Once a ferry route has been decided, get the brochures from all the companies who make that crossing, compare costs and see what each provides in the way of entertainment. A cinema is useful on a long journey, some boats have discos, and The Sally Line, which went into service in 1981, offers passengers the use of two saunas during the two- to three-hour crossing from Ramsgate to Dunkirk. Brittany Ferries is said to serve good French food, while the Scandinavian lines are well known for the excellence of their service.

If you find the whole business of comparing prices, usually based on the length of car and the number of passengers, too tiresome to work out, you could look at the brochure put out by Ferrysave. This company, set up in 1981, offers a cross Channel booking package consisting of return fare, personal and medical insurance, motoring emergency and breakdown service, GB sticker and camping carnet. The brochure is very easy to follow as just one fare is quoted for each crossing, based on the car and the number of passengers listed above the price. As the company deals with the major ferry companies, quoting their names, prices and departure times it is easy for the prospective traveller to work out the most suitable crossing for his party.

FERRY CROSSINGS

Before booking a passage it is worth distinguishing between the three types of craft now used to ferry passengers across the Channel. There are the traditional ferry boats, motor vessels, some of which can now carry up to 1,300 passengers and 350 cars and many of which take heavy lorries, coaches and motor cycles as well as private cars. These motor vessels have a number of decks, snack bars or restaurants, a bar and often cabins. Passengers are able to move freely round the ship.

Hovercraft, and more recently jetfoils, are more like aircraft. Their crossings are known as flights and their passenger-carrying capacity is far less than traditional ferry boats. The big thing in their favour is their speed and, in the jetfoil, their smoothness.

The flat-bottomed Hovercraft, which have been in operation for over a decade, move on a cushion of air above the water and accommodate around 420 passengers and up to 55 cars. A hovercraft takes about 30 minutes to cross from Dover to Calais as opposed to the motor vessel time of about 1¼ hours. Passengers are not encouraged to move round during the flight.

Jetfoils, which have boat-like hulls, travel above the surface of the water and greatly cut down the ups and downs of sea crossing. B & I used jetfoils on their Liverpool to Dublin route, a notoriously choppy passage on a conventional ferry boat, for years but have now discontinued the service. Sealink introduced a jetfoil service from Dover to Ostend in 1981. Jetfoils owe their remarkable steadiness to the fact that, when out to sea, they are supported above the water by stilts equipped with underwater wings. Computers constantly monitor and adjust the position of the craft to keep it on an even keel. Jetfoils take just over 300 passengers on their two decks but as yet cannot accommodate cars. So while they are a boon to the holidaymaker looking for a quick European break they are not suitable for those travelling with a full car.

To help you decide which is the best crossing for your family, there follows a list of the approximate times taken for crossings from the British ports to the various continental ports they serve. Although the names of the ferry companies operating out of those ports have been included, the ferry situation is volatile, and not all the companies listed may still be in existence a year from the time of writing. Prices have not been quoted because, after the cut-throat war of the past few years, these can change two or three times even in one season. The ports are given in a clockwise list round Britain. Some, but not all, the companies given in the final column go to all the ports listed in the second column.

British port	Continental port	Time taken	Vessel used	Ferry companies
Newcastle	Bergen	19 hrs	All motor	DFDS (UK) Ltd
	Stavanger	18 hrs	vessels	Danish Seaways
	Kristiansand	20 hrs		
	Oslo	29 hrs		
	Gothenburg	25 hrs		
	Esbjerg	19 hrs		
Hull	Rotterdam	14 hrs	Motor vessel	P&O Ferries
	Zeebrugge	15 hrs		North Sea Ferries
Great Yarmouth	Scheveningen	8 hrs	Motor vessel	Norfolk Line
Felixstowe	Zeebrugge	5-8 hrs	Motor vessel	Townsend Thoresen
	Gothenburg	23 hrs		DFDS (UK) Ltd

British port	Continental port	Time taken	Vessel used	Ferry companies
Harwich	Hook of Holland	6-8 hrs	Motor vessel	Sealink
	Esbjerg	19 hrs		DFDS (UK) Ltd
	Bremerhaven	16 hrs		
	Hamburg	20 hrs		
	Kristiansand	23 hrs		
	Oslo	32 hrs		
Sheerness	Vlissingen	7 hrs	Motor vessel	Olau Line
Ramsgate	Calais	40 mins	Hovercraft	Hoverspeed
	Dunkirk	2½ hrs	Motor vessel	The Sally Line Ltd
Dover	Boulogne	1¾ hrs	Motor vessel	P&O Ferries
		35 mins	Hovercraft	Sealink
	Calais	1¼ hrs	Motor vessel	Townsend Thoresen
		35 mins	Hovercraft	Hoverspeed
	Dunkirk	2½ hrs	Motor vessel	Sealink
	Ostend	3½ hrs	Motor vessel	
		1½ hrs	Jetfoil	
	Zeebrugge	4-4½ hrs	Motor vessel	Townsend Thoresen
Folkstone	Calais	1¾ hrs	Motor vessel	Sealink
	Boulogne	1¾ hrs		
	Ostend	4½ hrs		
Newhaven	Dieppe	4 hrs	Motor vessel	Sealink
Portsmouth	Le Havre	5½ hrs	Motor vessel	Townsend Thoresen
	Cherbourg	4½ hrs		Brittany Ferries
	St Malo	8½ hrs		
Southampton	Le Havre	7-8 hrs	Motor vessel	P&O Ferries
	Cherbourg	5 hrs		Townsend Thoresen
Weymouth	Cherbourg	4 hrs	Motor vessel	Sealink
Plymouth	Roscoff	6 hrs	Motor vessel	Brittany Ferries
	Santander	22 hrs		
Pembroke	Rosslare	4 hrs	Motor vessel	B & I Line
	Cork	8-9 hrs		
Fishguard	Rosslare	3 hrs 40 mins	Motor vessel	Sealink
Holyhead	Dun Laoghaire	3½ hrs	Motor vessel	Sealink
Liverpool	Dublin	7-8 hrs	Motor vessel	B & I Line
Stranraer	Larne	2¼ hrs	Motor vessel	Sealink
Cairnryan	Larne	2-2½ hrs	Motor vessel	Townsend Thoresen

Holidaymakers travelling to the continent from Eire do not always have to travel to England first. There are two services operating directly from Eire to France.

Irish port	Continental port	Time taken	Vessel used	Ferry companies
Rosslare	Cherbourg	17 hrs	Motor vessel	Irish Continental
	Le Havre	20 hrs		Service
Cork	Roscoff	13 hrs	Motor vessel	Brittany Ferries

When it comes to packing the car, the rule is: heavy things, such as the cooker unit, the big gas container and the tent canvas, at the bottom of the boot. If you use a luggage rack it is well worth buying an all-over waterproof container specially made for roof racks: the cost starts at around £15. Plastic sheets kept down with elasticized cords are unsatisfactory for these eventually tear. The roof rack is the best place for flat things, such as chairs, tables, airbeds, and (if they are aluminium) the tent poles. All luggage racks have maker's recommended maximum loads which should be observed, and remember that the higher the luggage rack is piled, the greater the petrol consumption will be. Make sure that the picnic for the journey, a jersey or anorak for each occupant of the car and any books that will be needed on a cross-Channel ferry are easily accessible.

What to pack

Advice on the appropriate type of clothing to take on a camping holiday is given in Chapter 5. As far as the *volume* of clothing is concerned, keep it as low as possible. It is too easy, especially when travelling by car, to say, 'I'll take that, just in case,' but there is just not enough space. The rule is to be disciplined. Give careful thought to the number of days you will be away and the type of life you plan to lead on holiday. There is absolutely no need to take enough clean clothes for every day: clean clothes last longer when camping, especially if the family spends most of the day in swimming gear, and if a small amount of washing is done each day it is perfectly possible to have a 'one-off, one-on' system for clothes, certainly for adults and older children. This daily washing is not as tedious as it sounds and it does avoid having to cope with a mountain of dirty clothes on your return.

Space can, of course, be saved by sharing certain items. For example, pack one communal lightweight raincoat for night-time visits to the loo. Track suits, if the family uses them, are bulky but are useful after showers, so share one, otherwise take a sharing towelling bath robe. Mothers and daughters can share shower caps, and children can share a hairbrush.

For further advice on the type of clothes to take camping, see page 126.

For efficient packing it is, of course, helpful to make a list. Every family builds up its own camping list over the years. For first-timers, however, here is a list of basic items which you will need. It is useful to jot down in a notebook anything that has been omitted which may be useful on subsequent holidays. Ideally, double-check against your list both when assembling your equipment and when loading it into the car.

Camping equipment	Cooking and cleaning items	Miscellaneous items
Tent	Basic foodstuffs	Tent tidy
Groundsheet	Cutlery	Torches
Tent pegs	Crockery	Puncture repair kit
Mallets	Mugs	Tent patch repair kit
Cooker plus stand	Kettle	Coat hangers
Gas container	Wine glasses	String
Picnic stove	Cool box	Scissors
Barbecue	Freezer sachets	First-aid kit
Jet cleaners	Saucepan canteen	Sewing kit
Spare gas cartridges	Omelette pan	Safety pins
Lantern plus hook	Salad bowl	Sellotape
Matches	Wooden spoons	Mirror
Spare mantels	Small sharp knife	Sun umbrella
Strip light	Bread knife	Fly spray
Table	Chopping boards	Insect repellent
Chairs	Tin opener	Water purifiers
Airbeds/campbeds	Corkscrew	Toilet paper
Air pillows	Crown cap opener	Fire extinguisher
Inflator	Washing-up bowl	
Sleeping bags	Rubber gloves	
Spare blankets	Detergent	
Water carriers	Dish cloth	
	Tea towels	
	Pan scourer	
	Kitchen paper roll	
	Rubbish bags	
	Lidded buckets	
	Clothes line	
	Laundry bag	
	Clothes pegs	
	Clothes airer	
	String shopping bag	
	Dustpan and brush	

Miscellaneous personal	Car	Documentation
Sun-tan oil or cream	Warning triangle	Passports
Sun glasses	Emergency windscreen	Camping carnet
Sun hats	Spares kit	Money
Shampoo	Tow rope	Traveller's cheques
Camera	GB sticker	Insurance
Books	Chamois leather	Form E111 (for
Writing materials	Spare keys	reciprocal medical
Playing cards		treatment)
Badminton set		Green-card insurance
Clothes		Driving licence
Sports gear		Vehicle registration
Swimsuits		document
Towels		Tickets
Sandals		Phrase book
Flip-flops		Camp-site guide
		Dictionary
		Maps

Getting there and back

So the decision to go camping has been made. The equipment has been bought, borrowed or hired or a fully equipped tent rented on a European site. Those crossing the Channel have booked their passage, and everything is ready. Now comes what in some ways is the most exciting part of the whole adventure – getting to the final destination. If you have booked a coach/tent holiday you will not have the worry of having to drive yourself, but neither will you have the fun of working out the route. If you are travelling 'under your own steam', whether your destination is within Great Britain or abroad, the main ways of reaching it (now that air freighting cars has virtually disappeared) are road, Motorail, or a combination of the two. Plenty of people, of course, go backpacking or camping by bicycle, but as this book is aimed primarily at families, too encumbered to enjoy the complete freedom of the single traveller, only the less energetic methods of travel are dealt with here.

GETTING THERE BY ROAD: GREAT BRITAIN

Driving to a camp site in the British Isles needs almost as much attention as taking off for the continent, as anyone who has ever driven up to the north of Scotland will know. Once motorways are left behind, secondary roads, which increase in undulation the more they wind into hills or mountains, slow driving down to 48 kilometres (30 miles) an hour or less. It is important, therefore, to plan your journey realistically, allowing plenty of time for stops, shopping breaks, picnics, going to the lavatory or for simply admiring the view. Estimate all journeys, particularly with young children in the back of the car, on an average speed of 48 kilometres (30 miles) an hour. This sounds horribly slow, but it does allow for traffic jams, negotiating unknown towns, general hold-ups and rest periods. Even if there are no delays, it gives a psychological boost to arrive earlier than planned at a camp site.

In terms of comfort and general family happiness it is worth, even in England, planning for overnight stops on a long journey. The drive from London to Cornwall, for example, is quite exhausting when attempted in one day, especially in high summer when roads are crowded. Overnight stops avoid the bad-tempered early morning start and the exhausted late arrival. Experienced campers know that nothing damages good family relationships more, especially on the first day of a holiday which should be full of joyous expectation, than a late arrival at a site. Far better to arrive at a site, even an overnight one, in mid- to late afternoon. This gives plenty of time to unload, put up the tent, relax, explore and enjoy the evening.

OVERNIGHT STOPS IN GREAT BRITAIN

There are two schools of thought on overnight stops. Some campers do not mind the effort of getting all the equipment out, only to repack it next morning. They reckon that this is worth the trouble in view of the low cost of site fees and self-catering compared to hotel accommodation and meals.

Should you elect for a 'one night stand' at a camp site, remember that it is advisable to book ahead if you plan to travel at the weekend in the high holiday season, particularly if you will be camping in a popular area such as the Lake District, the Peak District, parts of Wales or the West Country. Remember also, however, that a growing number of sites will not accept one-night bookings at weekends in the high season. Most camp site managers who do allow one night stops will accept telephone bookings as long as they are immediately followed by written confirmation and a deposit. On the other hand, if you can manage to travel mid-week and be safely ensconced in your camp site when the Friday rush begins, you stand more chance of getting a 'casual' site for the night.

The second school of thought prefers to get bed and breakfast *en route* or stay in a small inn or farmhouse. Last summer campers paid between £10 and £20 for a family room, bed and breakfast.

For those who prefer to be surrounded by bricks and mortar during their overnight stop, the twelve regions of the English Tourist Board (addresses on page 85) have lists of accommodation in their 'Where to Stay' guides. There is also a number of yearly updated guides to guesthouses, farms, inns and similar accommodation on sale in most bookshops from March onwards.

OVERNIGHT STOPS ON THE CONTINENT

The policy of travelling mid-week applies just as much to the continent as to home. If you possibly can, avoid driving across France during the final weekend in July when the French holiday starts.

Booking overnight stops on the continent is not as simple as at home and on the whole is not advisable. For one thing, it is not always easy to calculate precise travelling distances; and for another, site managers, while they will often accept bookings for more than a few days, are not always too keen to lock up pitches for overnight stops that may not be claimed. It is possible for those renting a tent to have overnight accommodation on the journey, usually in small hotels, included as part of their package; for the independent traveller, however, there are three ways of coping with the problem.

First, if you plan to use your own equipment, you can just trust to luck and hope to get in somewhere. This slows the journey down a little as, for safety's sake, you should start looking for a site well before five o'clock. In France you will find that municipal sites are excellent value for overnight stops. As they are run by local authorities they are reasonably priced and the majority offer simple but clean and adequate facilities.

The second way of coping with the overnight-stop problem is to book with Mocamps, a unique organization set up specifically for the purpose. This British-based company offers overnight stops in fully equipped tents on seven sites spread strategically throughout France. Like other rent-a-tent companies, Mocamps has couriers on site and provides everything needed for an overnight stop, with the exception of personal bedding and cutlery. 'Proper' as opposed to campbeds are used in the main bedroom. Expect to pay between £11.50 and £19 a night, depending on the size of the family, the time of the year, and the day of the week. There is a supplement for the Paris site.

The third way of spending a night *en route* is to stay in small hotels or guesthouses. The French government tourist office produces an excellent annual publication, usually around March. *Logis de France*, lists over four thousand *logis, auberges* and rural hotels at charges ranging from £7 to £20. The book is free, but 50p is required to cover postage and packing. These small hotels, with their heavily papered and solidly comfortable bedrooms, which Madame always shows to guests before they book are full of the atmosphere of rural France which should be sampled at least once, even on a camping holiday.

114

Although overnight stops in France seem to receive most attention, probably because France is a large country and first choice with British campers, you may of course wish to break your journey in another country. Germany, for example, has an excellent tourist structure and local tourist offices can supply lists of camp sites and reasonably priced accommodation. The same is true of Belgium and the Netherlands.

Generally speaking, the problem of getting into camp sites, long-term or overnight, becomes worse the further south one goes. There is therefore a great deal to be said for camping in northern Europe, especially if the family dislikes crowds, enjoys walking and exploring and is not put off by a climate similar to our own.

GETTING THERE BY RAIL

If cost is not too important it might be worth considering using the Motorail service, either in this country or on the continent. British Rail has eighteen routes in the United Kingdom, the services to Scotland and the West Country being the most popular with summer holidaymakers. There are no longer any Motorail links to British ports. In the high season during the summer of 1982 the single second-class fare from London to St Austell for a family of four, parents and two children under sixteen and their car was £85, the return fare was £138. However, in the low season the same five hour journey cost £58 single and £107 return. Since last year daytime Motorail passengers travelling to and from Cornwall have used one of the fast 125 Intercity trains, their cars travelling separately. For summer 1983 new air-conditioned and sound-proofed sleeping cars will be introduced on the London to Stirling and Inverness overnight Motorail services.

Generally, cars, which are chained to a special wagon when travelling by Motorail, must not be higher than 2.15 m (7 ft) including the luggage rack. This rule also applies to the continental Motorail.

In Europe you can transport your car to places as distant as Lisbon or Munich by rail, or to Avignon, Biarritz, Marseilles, Nice or Fréjus. In 1982 a new route started, from Boulogne to Brive, ideal for those camping in the Dordogne region or central France. The majority of British campers using Motorail make for the Mediterranean on an overnight service. In summer 1982 a family of four, with two children under eleven, paid £227.50 for a single second-class Motorail ticket from Dover to Avignon, excluding sleeping accommodation. There is a reduction for return fares.

Initially, Motorail charges may seem high, particularly those to the Mediterranean, but when compared with the cost of petrol, motorway tolls, overnight stops and general wear and tear on the family, they appear in a different light.

Many families prefer to take the Motorail one way, usually at the start of the holiday. It can be a better idea, however, to travel back by train, when the fun and anticipation have gone out of the holiday and the prospect of camping in northern France, where it always seems to be raining by the end of August, is not enticing.

Motorails tend to get booked early for the summer months, both here and abroad. Timetables come out in the early spring, so if you are considering putting your car on the train, book in plenty of time. British timetables should be available from travel agents, if you experience any difficulty in obtaining the continental timetable write to the French Railways (SNCF) office in this country (address page 119).

FINAL ADVICE BEFORE DEPARTURE

The last few days before going on any self-catering holiday are always hectic because so much has to be left until the last minute. The final few days before a camping holiday on which you are planning to use your own equipment are even worse because of the amount of gear that has to be assembled.

It really is not necessary to clean the house thoroughly as well as going on holiday. Forget about defrosting the refrigerator, cleaning the oven, washing the kitchen floor and tending the garden. There is enough to do washing clothes, arranging for neighbours to take care of animals and plants, remembering to cancel the milk and papers and to unplug the television set without beating yourself into the ground with a mini spring clean.

For families there is a considerable advantage in starting a holiday on a Monday rather than a Friday, as has been customary in the past. Now that holidays are longer and many employers will allow staggered leaves, it makes for a much more relaxed start to have a weekend at home to do the packing together. It is when one partner assumes that the other has packed a particular item that things get left behind, especially on that late Friday dash.

If you have booked in at fixed sites, give the address and telephone number to neighbours and relatives. If you have not made any bookings but plan to travel freely, ring home occasionally. Most European countries have coin boxes that dial through to Britain.

Finally, make a last check of the house, ensuring that doors are locked, windows closed, electric appliances unplugged and heating turned off. Get in the car and relax. After all, you are going off on holiday.

Addresses

Tent repair companies

Aquarian,
Phoenix Works,
500 King Street,
Longton,
Stoke-on-Trent,
Staffs. ST3 1EZ.

**C F Barker and Sons
(Marquees) Ltd,**
259 London Road,
Croydon,
Surrey.

Barretts of Feckenham,
Feckenham,
Redditch,
Worcs.

G.T.S. Camping Ltd,
Unit 3,
Barnet Trading Estate,
Barnet,
Herts.

Pointnorth,
4 Gwelfor,
Cemaes Bay,
Anglesey,
Gwynedd.

Cheshire Camp & Leisure,
Evans House,
Norman Street,
Warrington,
Cheshire.

Tent Valeting Services,
3rd Floor, Grecian Mill,
Worsley Mill,
Worsley Road North,
Worsley,
Manchester.

Burton Tent and Camp Hire,
121 Branston Road,
Burton-on-Trent,
Staffs.

The Camping Repair Centre,
163 Fishponds Road,
Eastville,
Bristol,
Avon.

The Protective Textile Co. Ltd,
Barge Walk,
East Molesey,
Surrey KT8 9AL.

For made-to-measure eyeletted
groundsheets.

City Hardware,
6-8 Goswell Road,
London EC1.
For repairing lights, cookers and so on, but not for tents.

Maps

John Bartholomew & Son Ltd,
Duncan Street,
Edinburgh EH 9 1TA.

Ordnance Survey,
Southampton,
Hants.

Wm. Collins Sons & Co. Ltd,
14 St James's Place,
London SW1A 1PS.

Michelin Tyre Co,
Michelin House,
81 Fulham Road,
London SW3 6RD.

Passport Office,
Clive House,
Petty France,
London SW1H 9HD.

McCarta Ltd,
122 King's Cross Road,
London WC1X 9DS.

Stanfords Ltd,
12-14 Long Acre,
London WC2E 9LP.

GB Car Club,
PO Box 11,
Romsey,
Hants SO5 8XX.

The AA,
Fanum House,
Basingstoke,
Hants RG21 2EA.

Grangersol Ltd,
Imperial Way,
Watford,
Herts.

There are also passport offices in Peterborough, Liverpool, Glasgow, Newport and Belfast. The addresses are given on passport application forms; these are obtained from main post offices.

Insurance

British Insurance Brokers Association,
130 Fenchurch Street,
London EC3.

Fennel, Turner & Taylor Ltd,
Pinners Hall,
Autin Friars,
London EC2P 2HS.

West Mercia Brokers,
High Street,
Wombourne,
Nr Wolverhampton,
West Midlands WV5 9ND.

Europa Insurance Co Ltd,
Rothschild House,
Whitgift Centre,
Croydon CR9 1NP.

Europ Assistance,
252 High Street,
Croydon CR0 1NF.

British Insurance Association,
PO Box 538,
Aldemay House,
Queen Street,
London EC4N 1TU.

Ferry companies

North Sea Ferries Ltd,
King George Dock,
Hedon Road,
Hull HU9 5QA.

Norfolk Line,
Atlas House,
Southgate Road,
Great Yarmouth,
Norfolk.

Townsend Thoresen,
European Ferries Group,
Dover,
Kent CT16 3BR.

Sealink,
Eversholt House,
163/203 Eversholt Street,
London NW1.

Olau Line,
Sheerness,
Kent ME12 1SN.

Irish Continental Service,
19/21 Aston Quay,
Dublin 2,
Eire.

Hoverspeed,
International Hoverport,
Ramsgate,
Kent CT12 5HS.

Sally Line Ltd,
Ramsgate Harbour,
Kent CT11 8RP.

Brittany Ferries,
Norman House,
Kettering Terrace,
Albert Johnson Quay,
Portsmouth PO2 7AE.

P&O Ferries,
Arundel Towers,
Portland Terrace,
Southampton SO9 4AE.

B & I Line,
155 Regent Street,
London W1R 7FD.

French Railways Ltd (SNCF),
179 Piccadilly,
London W1V 0BA.

French Government Tourist Office,
178 Piccadilly,
London W1V 0AL.

Ferrysave Tours Ltd,
1 Nugent Terrace,
London NW8 9QB.

DFDS (UK) Ltd,
Latham House,
16 Minories,
London EC3N 1AN.
This line now incorporates Danish Seaways, Prins Ferries, Fred. Olsen Lines and Sessan Tor Line.

5
Life on a Camp Site

What to do on arrival

When you arrive at the camp site of your choice, you will have to check in at reception, whether you have booked or not. Procedure is fairly standard: you will be expected to give the number of people in your group, the ages of the children, if any, whether you have a tent or a caravan and how long you intend to stay. Generally, in Europe you will have to complete a simple form stating your name, address, occupation and passport number. Some camp site wardens still hold on to your passport or camping carnet as proof of identification until you leave, but this practice seems to be dying out.

Once you have been allocated a pitch you will be shown where to go. Depending on the sophistication of the site, you will either be taken, sometimes by a guide on foot, on a bicycle or moped, to the allotted place – common practice on sites where pitches are marked out – or you will be told where to go and left to find your own way – more usual where pitches are not marked out and where campers may put up their tents where they wish within a certain area.

If you have not been shown where the washrooms, shop and cold water supply are, find out before putting up the tent. If you have any choice in the matter, you may wish to change your pitch slightly – for example, you may not want to be too close to the toilet block if you like a peaceful existence!

On Mediterranean sites, particularly if you have small children in your party, it is advisable to seek more shade than when camping in England. Even though tents, particularly when the sides can be rolled up or opened out to give a through breeze, are a good deal cooler than caravans, they can still be pretty hot, especially the inner compartments if the afternoon sun has been beating on them. In hot climates, therefore, it is sensible to pitch the tent where it receives partial, not deep, shade in the afternoon and early evening.

Finding the best pitch

On the more formally organized sites you may not be able to choose your pitch: the proprietor or warden may allocate one to you. However, it is possible to choose a bad pitch even on an official site, so if you have the opportunity, select with care. Find out the direction of the prevailing wind and face away from it;

decide whether you want the morning or evening sun and pitch accordingly. This is particularly important in valley camps where sometimes the sun does not reach one slope till well after noon. A pitch on a flat headland may command beautiful views of the sea, but one further back will be more sheltered. A pitch close to a river or stream might be fine for swimming, but if the ground is marshy the tent might flood in the first downpour.

It should be remembered that most camp-site guide books are prepared for both tent campers and caravanners, and it is the camper with a tent who must pay particular attention to the terrain. A grassy slope is far more of an obstacle to comfort to those who have to cope with tent pegs and slipping sleeping bags than it is to caravanners who can adjust the legs of their mobile home. A flat pitch is essential for a tent, not only because it makes sleeping more comfortable, but also because a tent frame set on uneven ground can distort, the canvas will not sit properly and the zips, taking too much strain, can break.

The daily routine

Life on a camp site seems to be an unexplained mystery to non-campers. There is a widely held, but mistaken belief, that campers have to spend all their time putting up tents, then taking them down again, carrying heavy water carriers from distant taps, going on time-consuming shopping expeditions and then having to spend what little free time is left cooking gigantic meals in difficult conditions.

Nothing could be further from the truth. Any visitor to a camp site, either in this country or abroad, would immediately get an overall impression of leisure; people quietly going about following the occupations that interest them most, reading, playing tennis, swimming or gently walking round the site inspecting other people's equipment, a favourite and innocent pastime this and a good way of getting ideas for improving one's own 'outfit'. Putting up a tent and getting all the gear neatly stowed away inside is a job that experienced campers accomplish in under an hour; those renting a tent just walk into fully furnished accommodation, so that leaves plenty of time for leisure activities. Incidentally, when it comes to housework campers fare better than other self-caterers. With a rented tent all you need is to nip round with the dustpan and brush provided by the company an hour or so before you leave, check that the cooker and cool box are clean and empty and make sure that nothing has been left under the beds. Even when camping with your own gear packing up need not take too long if it is 'all hands to the pump'.

To get the best out of the daily routine it is worth finding out and avoiding the peak times for queues at the shop, showers and, for men, at the wash basins for the early morning shave. Early risers score on all counts. There is only a handful of men shaving at around 7.30 a.m., while the queues for bread and milk only begin to get long after the shop has been open for an hour.

If you take a seaside holiday it pays to leave the beach an hour or so before the general drift back. Then you can shower immediately, there will be no queues and plenty of hot water and the floor of the cubicle will not be sandy. If you do not mind tramping from tent to toilet block in the dark, the showers are often empty last thing at night. Check that the electricity is not turned off at a certain time each night. Families often find it more convenient to take small children to be showered and to have their hair washed after lunch – always a quiet time at the showers. This is also a good time for washing clothes (mid-morning is quite the worst). In fact as most campers seem to follow their home routine on site all you have to do to avoid the crush is to alter your timing slightly to avoid clashing with the crowd.

As to what people actually do during the day when camping, that is very much up to the individual. Some are rarely seen on site, using the tent merely as a base for pursuing other interests. Others seem to spend the entire day around the camp. Most families come mid way between these extremes, having the occasional day out, perhaps at the beach, then every now and then an 'in' day to catch up with chores, postcard writing and so on. A day on site is generally no hardship for children. Good sites have sturdy perimeter fences and usually only one main entrance, so children should come to no harm if left to their own devices for an hour or two. In fact when there are other children to play with, sports facilities, play areas and games and television rooms to occupy them, it can sometimes be difficult to drag them away for a day out.

Long leisurely meals, particularly in the evenings when the night is fine and the day has been spent in the open, are a highlight of camping. This is one of the reasons why camp cooking should be enjoyable rather than a burden.

Cooking

Simplicity is the key to successful camp cooking, and because self-catering is reasonably inexpensive it is possible to allow occasional treats, or sometimes to buy the main part of the evening meal from the camp take-away, if there is one.

Cooking under canvas, or preferably completely in the open, is one of the pleasures of camping, chiefly because there is so much more time to spare than at home. Unusual meals are all part of the holiday enjoyment so try using local produce as much as possible. Most campers are quite content to exist on one hot meal a day, and even then salads and bread or rice can replace vegetables. Rice is a particularly useful holiday food because it needs no preparation and any left-overs can be used as the basis for a salad or kedgeree the next day.

Most people find that camping, even in the warm Mediterranean climate, makes them a lot hungrier than at home; camping in a cold climate makes people positively ravenous. It is sensible, therefore, to get the day off to a good start with a substantial breakfast. Having eaten well at the beginning of the day, you will find that only a light lunch is needed.

Traditionalists may feel that they are letting the family down if they do not cook a standard English dinner every evening, but this is unnecessary provided that the food is nutritionally sound. It is also naturally important that meals are varied, and it is not too difficult to find a number of different but simple-to-cook foods for the evening meal. For example, there are plain or filled omelettes, grilled, fried or barbecued chops, a mixed grill, grilled or fried fish, or even *moules marinières*. Hamburgers go down well, but they have to be home-made if you are camping abroad as frozen ones are not generally available in continental supermarkets – but they are, of course, tastier when freshly made. Vegetables on their own can also make a tasty main course if preceded by, say, melon and followed by cheese, peaches, and then a shared large bar of chocolate. Ratatouille, too, makes an excellent main course. Then there are salads, such as *salade Niçoise*, which can be a meal in themselves.

With so much fresh fruit available in the summer, both in Britain and abroad, it really is not necessary to make conventional puddings. A simple main course preceded by a starter such as melon, stuffed tomatoes, eggs, pâté or just a selection of chopped raw vegetables, and followed by fruit and cheese makes a delicious, nutritional meal which requires very little preparation.

For those who still need inspiration there are a number of excellent cookery books available. These are listed on page 187.

WHAT TO TAKE: FOOD AND COOKING EQUIPMENT

As the cost of food in this country has now caught up with Continental prices, there is no point in taking other than basics, such as salt, pepper, coffee and tea, and those for the sake of convenience rather than for economic reasons. Although it might not seem sensible to use up precious storage space in the car unnecessarily, if you are camping with small children it is also worth taking supplies of a favourite food which is unavailable in the country for which you are bound – this can make quite a difference to their enjoyment of the holiday.

Although cooking equipment may be provided for those renting a tent, they should check carefully beforehand exactly what is supplied and make good any deficiency themselves. People camping with their own equipment are advised to use the list on page 111 as a guide to the cooking utensils they will need.

One 'extra' piece of equipment which is well worth having is a barbecue. These have been discussed in Chapter 1.

Shopping

Find out the opening times of the local shops (see Chapter 6 for guidance). All over the continent local feast days can be disconcertingly celebrated, so check at camp reception before setting off. Many shops close down completely for a week or a fortnight in the summer, but if one bread shop in town has a holiday notice up there is bound to be another open elsewhere. During the summer the BBC gives details of continental public holidays as well as traffic and weather conditions in its 'Going Places' programme on Radio 4 after the six o'clock news bulletin on Friday evenings. Further weather reports and the state of traffic on the continental roads, as well as information on new sections of motorway and comments on the cross-Channel ferries, are given at the start of the 'Breakaway' programme, also on Radio 4, on Saturday mornings after the nine a.m. news bulletin.

Shopping on holiday can be very enjoyable, particularly in local markets, which are every bit as good in Great Britain as on the continent. Because these markets are so colourful the danger is to buy more than you can eat before it spoils, so make a list and stick to it. Remember that the best buys in continental markets are cheeses (the hard varieties keep better than the soft), nuts and dried fruits (excellent in salads and as nutritious snacks) and of course local fresh fruit and vegetables and, where it is available, local fish.

Try to get to the market fairly early in the morning as most finish around lunchtime; besides, perishable goods are always fresher bought early in the day. Very small villages tend to have only one market day a week, larger towns may have them twice or three times a week, while the big cities, particularly in Italy and Spain, often have daily markets. The camp reception may be able to provide details.

Basics such as butter, cooking oil, eggs, wine and so on, are best bought at supermarkets or at the camp shop if the prices are reasonable. It is always more convenient to buy milk from the camp shop.

In France glass wine bòttles and certain fizzy-drink bottles have deposits on them, so remember to return them to the shop. *Vin ordinaire*, recognizable for its astonishing cheapness (30p to 80p a bottle) and the fact that it often comes in a plastic bottle and always has a cap instead of a cork, is fine for everyday drinking. However, it is worth trying the wines of the region you are in. Many of these may not travel and will therefore not be available at home, so enjoy them while you can.

Finally, if you can carry one, a dictionary or a copy of *Shopping and Cooking in Europe* (see the Bibliography) will prove useful when you go shopping.

Camp clothing

The most important thing about camp clothes is that they be comfortable and reasonably loose, for there is plenty of bending and stretching involved in putting up a tent. Even rent-a-tenters may find that they move round more than they do on other holidays. Clothes made of natural fibres, or a mixture of natural and man-made fibres are better than those made entirely of synthetics. Cotton and wool are cooler in hot and warmer in cold weather than all man-made materials.

The golden rule is to be prepared for both hot and cold weather wherever you go. Long-sleeved shirts and blouses, as well as cotton trousers, will be useful to avoid sunburn if a whole day is to be spent on the beach, whether at home or abroad, where the sun can still be very hot. Campers heading for the Mediterranean should take a shirt or dress that unbuttons all the way down, as struggling to pull a garment with only a couple of buttons at the neck-opening down over a sunburnt back is quite agonizing. And *always* make sure you have a sunhat.

Jerseys are essential wherever you go, for even in the Mediterranean evenings can be chilly, while that old English favourite, the trusty cardigan, is very useful on a camping holiday. Remember, however, that heavier clothing is not easy to wash on a camp site, so do not bring light-coloured bulky garments which quickly become dirty.

Every member of the family needs a pair of comfortable walking shoes and sandals that are not too new. Feet, suddenly bare, can become blistered if new sandals are worn for the first time on holiday. Children will want to take their beloved training shoes, but persuade them that flip-flops are best for walking on very hot sand and for trips to the shower. At least one pair of wellingtons per family, particularly in England (perhaps not so essential in the Mediterranean), is useful for early morning walks to the camp shop when the grass can be heavy with dew. In fact, shoes for all the family form such a bulky item of camping luggage that the best way of transporting them is to put them together in a large strong carrier (a plastic laundry bag is good) rather than have them taking up space in suitcases.

There is a huge selection of jackets, cagoules, quilted waistcoats and anoraks available these days. In fact, the popularity of sports gear, much of it becoming fashion gear, has done a great deal to brighten up life on a camp site. Today jackets are available in delightful pastel colours and a wide range of styles, and excellent lightweight fillers that give warmth without bulk are used for linings. Some people like to wear thick jerseys or quilted waistcoats when the weather is cool, with lightweight waterproof cagoules for wet weather, while others prefer the more fashionable blousons; but beware of high fashion, for it is not always functional. Whatever your choice, you will probably need plenty of pockets.

Finally, people who feel the cold may want to take thermal underwear with them on a camping trip. There are some excellent makes available, one of the best-known being Damart, a company which also manufactures sweaters, socks, gloves and other warm clothing. Chain stores have now started to sell thermal underwear; remember to buy any items you need the winter before you go camping, they may not be in stock during the summer. Good thermal jackets are available from Fairway Technical-Plastics. These are sonic-welded, instead of being stitched, to give good windproofing, and are made from woven nylon with Dacron or Terylene fillings. As well as two quilted jackets, selling at around £10 each, the company also makes undergarments – clothes to make an extra layer between conventional underwear and outer garments.

Remember that whatever clothes you buy should be as suitable for home as for camping wear.

The weather

It is totally impossible to generalize about the weather other than to say that, on the whole, southern Europe is hotter than southern Britain. Camping holidays are, of course, particularly vulnerable to the weather, and whereas a couple of days torrential rain can be merely a nuisance to a family under a concrete roof, it can be a disaster to a unprepared one under canvas. It is therefore essential to be ready for bad weather, whether camping at home or abroad – and this means taking more than warm clothes and a couple of pair of boots: it means having something to occupy the family when walking or swimming is out of the question. So be sure to have a supply of board games, playing cards, paperbacks and writing materials. Reading aloud in turn is a good way of passing the time, even when the children are quite old.

Fortunately, there are few days when it is totally impossible to leave the tent. If the rain is intermittent, sight-seeing excursions can be arranged – in fact, it is best always to use poor weather for such expeditions and keep the fine days for the beach.

From a practical point of view, listen to the weather bulletins when holidaying in Britain, and to a certain extent in Europe. Now that Radio 4 is being broadcast on long wave it is possible to pick up the meteorological forecasts quite far into France and Germany on the car radio. This is useful in summer when the continental weather forecast is given on a number of bulletins, particularly at weekends. It is also worth buying local papers for weather bulletins on the continent: as maps with symbols are often used, it does not matter if you do not understand the language.

As well as rain, winds can be quite disturbing to campers, and there are more winds than many people realise in the Mediterranean region. The most famous, the Mistral, blows mainly in the winter and spring and is a cold dry strong wind. It blows along the Italian and French Mediterranean coast, from Marseille to Perpignan particularly, and can reach gale force as it funnels down the Rhône valley. On average the Mistral blows 100 days in the year, though once 170 days were recorded in Marseille. Closer to the Spanish border in the western Mediterranean, the wind is known as the Tramontane, literally 'across the mountain'. This blows off the Pyrenees and can be cold and unpleasant, especially when it whips and stings round bare legs.

One advantage to camping with one's own gear is that it is possible to beat the weather to a certain extent by striking camp and quickly moving on to an area where you know the weather to be good. All those who have put up with difficult camping conditions will recognize the feeling of complete well-being when at last the sun appears. It is moments such as these, not all that rare, that make camping worthwhile.

Addresses

Camp clothes

Damart Ltd,
Bingley,
West Yorkshire BD16 3ZD.

Fairway Technical-Plastics Ltd,
Battersea Road,
Heaton Mersey Industrial Estate,
Stockport,
Cheshire SK4 3EP.

Weather reports

London Weather Centre,
Penderel House,
284 High Holborn,
London WC1.
Tel. 01-836 4311

Although all regional weather enquiries can be answered at this office, there is a list of individual numbers for most of the country listed at the back of local code books. For camping in Great Britain it makes sense to use the local offices, checking with the London office for weather near the Channel ports.

6
What Each Country Has to Offer

It would be impossible for anyone to report with detailed first-hand knowledge on what European countries with camping facilities have to offer holidaymakers. In the following pages factual information is given on driving regulations, bank opening hours, the type of camp-site facilities available, the weather that can be expected and other facts which might be helpful to the camper. As over four million of us camp in the British Isles, with just over half a million Britons going abroad to camp, more space is devoted to Britain than to European countries. Countries are listed in order of popularity with British campers, rather than alphabetically.

Great Britain
It seems appropriate that camping began in this country (just before the First World War in fact) for when the weather is good camping in the British Isles is unbeatable.

Today there are over five hundred tourist information offices throughout the British Isles, many of which can provide up-to-date information on camp-site vacancies as well as on what to do and see in their areas. To avoid the rut that many campers can slide into of always making for a well-known and popular seaside resort, one of the national parks or other well known holiday areas send away for some of the major publications issued by each of the twelve regional tourist boards and by the Scottish, Wales and Northern Ireland tourist offices. Some of these guides have been discussed in Chapter 3.

With camping becoming more popular each year it is sensible to consider making for some of the lesser known, but nonetheless attractive, parts of the British Isles. Some of the countryside of Northern Ireland, for example, is staggeringly beautiful, with over 480 kilometres (300 miles) of coastline, much of it far from crowded and never more than an hour's drive from most inland places. There is a large number of forests in the province, some of them with excellent camping facilities and, with only about twenty cars per mile of road as compared to about sixty-six for Great Britain as a whole, driving is no great strain.

Northumberland has a fine coastline, as well as some outstandingly beautiful scenery inland. The Camping Club, many of whose sites accept non-members, has a couple of sites in this part of the world. A seaside site in an Area of Outstanding Natural

Beauty is at the small fishing village of Beadnell; the other, reserved for members only, some 12 kilometres (8 miles) from Alnwick, also in an Area of Outstanding Natural Beauty is within easy reach of the sea. Alan Rogers mentions an agreeable-sounding site developed by the local council along the banks of the River Wansbeck about 6 kilometres (4 miles) from the sea at Newbiggin. There are also Trax sites on the racecourses at Hexham and Newcastle.

Moving a little further south, there is enough space in North Yorkshire to absorb any amount of campers. Here an enterprising private concern, Freedom of Ryedale (address on page 173), provides a total service to holidaymakers. This organization, which acts as a back-up service to the local tourist office, will provide lists of self-catering accommodation from camp sites to cottages. It can also arrange cycle hire, pony trekking, fishing licences, deep-sea fishing trips, tours of the moors, visits to such famous abbeys as Fountains, Rievaulx and Kirkham, and 'wildwatching' days in the National Park. People writing for camping information will be sent a pack containing about twenty brochures of camp sites in the area.

The Heart of England is another marvellous area for a non-seaside camping holiday. There is a very fine well-run site at Leedons Park, just outside Broadway on the A44 leading to Evesham. Tent pitches are flat and grassy and toilets clean, and in 1982 the proprietor, Roy Parry, installed baths and deep dish-washing sinks as well as facilities for the disabled. There is a television and games room for when the weather is bad, a swimming pool and a well-stocked shop sophisticated enough to sell wine. Campers from Holland, Germany, France and Scandinavia as well as the British Isles use this site, which is open all the year round, as a base for making daily trips as far afield as London.

The Camping Club has two sites in the area, both for members only. One at Romsey is close to the Clent Hills, a National Trust property, the other is at Wolverley alongside the old Worcestershire/Staffordshire canal. For those planning to camp in Staffordshire the site at Trentham Gardens not far from Stoke-on-Trent is said to be exceptionally pleasant.

Another very rewarding holiday area is the Forest of Dean, where the Forestry Commission has four sites. The Grade A one at Christchurch, with hot showers and a camp shop, is recommended. The Monnow Bridge camp site at Monmouth has a good atmosphere and facilities, while it is generally reckoned that the Trax site at Chepstow is one of the best-run racecourse sites in the country. The Cottage Caravan park, which also takes tents, has a good reputation, and is awarded three pennants by the AA, is on the outskirts of Ross-on-Wye.

Moving into central and south Wales, there is beautiful scenery, both for driving and walking, in the National Park and National Trust areas of the Brecon Beacons and the Black Mountains. The Mountain Centre in the Brecon Beacons, just off the A740 a few miles south-west of Brecon, is not nearly as tough as the name suggests and provides a rest place for walkers or those on car excursions. It is a pleasant Scandinavian-style building open throughout the year with excellent toilet facilities, a comfortable lounge, heating in winter and a lovely picnic area with sturdy tables, comfortable chairs, and a wonderful view towards the Brecons. There is a snack bar for those who have not brought their own picnics and an information shop that sells maps, guides, and so on. There is plenty of car parking space and the centre makes an excellent base for either a day's walking or a half-hour stroll.

I have heard good reports of two sites in the Brecon Beacons, one at Talgarth, the other at Bronllys. The AA awards four pennants to the Talgarth site and advises booking in the high season. The opinion of the Letts guide is that the coastal sites are better equipped than the inland ones in this area.

Campers planning to visit Scotland might like to know of the South-West Scotland Holiday Parks Association. This organization, formed fourteen years ago, is a group of thirty site owners in the Dumfries and Galloway area who have banded together to offer well equipped and maintained sites. Although most are called 'parks' the majority accept tents.

Three seaside sites that personal experience has proved to be good are Lady's Mile Farm at Dawlish, Salcombe Regis Caravanning and Camping Site and Tregarton Farm Caravan and Camping Park at Gorran, Cornwall. Lady's Mile Farm, which merits three pennants in the AA guide, is beautifully run and scrupulously clean. It boasts hot showers, a good big laundry room and a well stocked shop. The area round the swimming pool is always tidy and the atmosphere excellent. It has a games and television room.

The Salcombe Regis Caravanning and Camping Site does not belong to the top facility class, but the site itself, being on a cliff top, is most attractive and the atmosphere pleasant.

Tregarton Farm Caravan and Camping Park at Gorran is also a cliff-top site. The AA currently rates it with three pennants and it now has a children's playground, a laundrette and a pub.

As there are some 3,000 camp sites open to the public in Great Britain from which to choose, it helps to have other opinions to back up the factual information given in the site guides. The three monthly publications that deal with camping, *Practical Camper, Camping* and the AA's *Drive & Trail*, all include very helpful features on sites that have been visited by experienced campers. *Practical Camper*'s 'What site?' features anything from two to five sites per issue and covers continental as well as British camps. *Camping*'s 'Sitescene' is similar, while *Drive & Trail* offers an annual Camp Site of the Year Award. For this the country is divided into six regions, and eighteen sites (three from each region) are selected as finalists. As the competition progresses, details of the eighteen selected sites are published in the magazine.

The 1981 winner, the Old Manor Caravan Park at Grafham in Cambridgeshire, makes an excellent base for exploring this quiet and picturesque part of England. The lodge in which the owners, Mr and Mrs Connelly, live is said at one time to have belonged to Oliver Cromwell. The site, set in over 2 hectares (6½ acres) of grounds, with its tiled toilet block, swimming pool, children's playground and shop, is a very good family site.

Unfortunately, it is easy for the inexperienced camper to pick a bad site, especially in a crowded and popular resort in peak holiday time. Beware particularly of unlicensed sites known as 'twenty-eight-day sites' – those where a landowner may allow any number of tents on a piece of land of 2 hectares (5 or more acres) for up to twenty-eight days in a year without needing planning permission or a licence. It is in the very popular areas of the country that this rule can be abused and campers may be charged high rates and receive very little in return. There are times when the authorities have to turn a blind eye to mild abuses of the twenty-eight-day rule, for what is the alternative in a very crowded holiday area when people may not camp on the roadside, in lay-bys or in public parks?

Until legislation is introduced to deal with this problem, how should campers recognize and avoid unlicensed sites? To begin with they should read the notice posted outside the camp, and if there is none they should go inside and ask for details. The majority of site proprietors, some 2,000 or so who take their operation seriously, as opposed to people who just let off land for camping as a side-line, belong to the National Federation of Site Operators. There is a code of conduct for members of this voluntary organization and – important from the camper's point of view – any complaints from the public against members are noted and dealt with. Over forty members of the National Federation of Site Operators have banded together to issue a small leaflet giving details of their sites.

If a site is not a member of the federation, check whether it is affiliated to the AA, the RAC or one of the camping clubs or if it is registered with the local tourist office. If the site fulfils any of these requirements, you will be certain at least of basic standards of hygiene.

It says much for the enterprise and the positive attitude of some site proprietors that in 1980 six of them banded together to publish a brochure, *The Best of British*. Their sites, which vary from large to small and which stretch from Scotland to Cornwall, have in common the fact that they are all individually run and well managed and that they keep their toilet and washing facilities up to a very high standard. One of the organizers said that they hope to expand the scheme over the next few years but never to have more than twenty sites under their umbrella. The ten camps now in the scheme, one of which was the first winner of the AA's Camp Site of the Year Award, are listed on page 173. Do not be put off by the words 'caravan park'; all ten sites accept tents.

A final word on British camp sites. A number now charge by the 'unit' instead of per person, which makes costing and administration easier. A unit consists of one tent or caravan, one car, two adults, one child over ten and one child under ten. This is the average; charges will obviously vary for smaller or larger families. In 1982 the average cost of a unit was between £2 and £4 a night.

There has been a steady improvement over the past decade in the standards of British camp sites. They may not all be as stylish as some of the big continental ones, but there is never any question about the standard of the drinking water or the plumbing – quite an important consideration.

The new wave of proprietors is keen and takes its duties seriously. The owners visit sites abroad for guidance and improve their own sites whenever it is financially possible; but, as one owner said, 'It takes quite a few camping nights to earn the £50,000 needed to put in a new toilet block'. However, dish-washing facilities, so common on the continent, have now been installed on a number of sites in this country, and others are following suit. Another continental practice, marked pitches for tents, is catching on over here. Many people prefer the freedom of being allowed to pitch a tent wherever they wish on a big flat grassy field, but there is a lot to be said for separate pitches. For one thing it means that the proprietor knows exactly where individual parties are – particularly useful in emergencies. Marked pitches also give a reasonable guarantee of space to the occupiers. It can be extremely irritating when, on a large and comparatively empty field, fellow campers pitch their tent only yards from yours. The irritation is heightened by the fact that you have no good reason for asking them to move over a bit. There is no danger of this happening with marked-out pitches.

Europe
DRIVING ON THE CONTINENT

As the majority of campers going abroad will be using the family car they will need to know something about traffic conditions and regulations in Europe. The most obvious difference to become accustomed to is, of course, driving on the right, but there are many more. Some general advice is given here and, where necessary, further detailed information is given under the heading for individual countries. However, campers with cars are strongly recommended to read the AA publication *Travellers' Guide in Europe*. This costs £3.95, is published annually in March and deals most comprehensively with the traffic regulations in force in the major European countries. It is particularly useful to have this book to hand when trying to park in a foreign city. The AA's *Camping and Caravanning in Europe*, already mentioned under camp site guide books, deals most comprehensively with European traffic regulations.

First, a general comment on motorways. There are no charges for motorways in Germany, Belgium, Luxembourg, the Netherlands or Scandinavia. Tolls are charged on most motorways in France, Italy, Spain and on sections of the Austrian, Greek, Portuguese and Yugoslavian motorways. The AA produces leaflets, available to members only, giving the tollway charges made by individual countries.

Lights
Dipped headlights should be used in conditions of fog, snow or heavy rain and when driving through a tunnel, irrespective of its length and lighting. In some cases police will wait at the end of a tunnel, checking that motorists are complying with this requirement.

Headlight flashing is generally used as a warning of approach or as a passing sign at night. In other circumstances it is accepted as a sign of annoyance or irritation and should be used with caution lest it be misunderstood.

Overtaking
When overtaking on roads with two lanes or more in each direction, always signal your intention in good time and after the manoeuvre signal and return to the inside lane. Do not remain in any other lane. Failure to comply with this regulation, particularly in France, will incur an on-the-spot fine (see under 'Police fines' below).

Always overtake on the left and use the horn as a warning to the driver of the vehicle being overtaken (except in areas where the use of the horn is prohibited). Do not overtake while being overtaken or when a vehicle behind is preparing to overtake. Do not overtake at level crossings, at intersections, the crest of a hill or at pedestrian crossings. When being overtaken, keep well to the right and reduce speed if necessary – never increase speed.

Parking

Parking is a problem nearly everywhere in Europe and police are extremely strict with offenders. Heavy fines are inflicted and unattended offending vehicles may be towed away. This can be both inconvenient and expensive, for heavy charges are imposed for the recovery of the impounded vehicles. In Athens number plates may be removed and confiscated from illegally parked vehicles. As a rule, always park on the right-hand side of the road or at an authorized place. As far as possible park off the main carriageway but not on cycle tracks, pedestrian verges or tram tracks.

Police fines

Police or on-the-spot fines can be imposed in one form or another by policemen in most countries in Europe. They are sometimes paid in cash to the policeman and sometimes at a post office against a 'ticket' issued by the policeman and always in the currency of the country concerned. Once paid they cannot be recovered. Such fines are intended to keep minor motoring offences out of courts, thus reducing administrative costs to the advantage of both motorists and police. Nevertheless, such fines are very high and punitive even for minor offences – they can range from £60 to £160. If the motorist disputes the charge he can opt to go before a court but this, in the case of a tourist, can lead to delays, inconvenience and extra expense. Further, as a guarantee of surety, particularly in more serious cases, the policeman is often authorized to demand a sum of money to cover anticipated fines and costs. If the depositing of cash is refused, the police officer is empowered to confiscate property or even the car to cover any deposits he thinks necessary. In most cases it is more straightforward to accept the fine. Remember always to obtain a receipt for deposits or fines.

Priority

The general rule is to give way to traffic entering from a junction to the right, but this is sometimes varied at roundabouts (see under 'Roundabouts' below). This is one aspect of European driving which may cause the British driver the most confusion because his whole training and experience makes it unnatural. Road signs indicate priority or loss of priority and tourists should make sure that they understand such signs. Great care should be taken at intersections and tourists should never rely on receiving the right of way, particularly in small towns or villages where local traffic, often slow-moving, such as farm tractors and so on, will assume right of way regardless of oncoming traffic. Always give way to public-service and military vehicles. Blind or disabled people, funerals and marching columns must also always be allowed right of way. Vehicles such as buses and coaches carrying large numbers of passengers will expect and should be allowed priority.

Road signs

Most road signs throughout Europe are internationally agreed and the majority would be familiar to the British motorist. Watch also for road markings – do not cross a solid white or yellow line marked on the road centre.

Roundabouts

Priority at roundabouts is given to vehicles entering the round-about unless signposted to the contrary. This is a complete reversal of the United Kingdom rule and particular care should be exercised when manoeuvring while circulating in an anti-clockwise direction on a roundabout. It is advisable to keep to the outside lane on a roundabout if possible, to make the exit easier.

Seat belts

Most of the countries mentioned in this book require visitors to wear seat belts. If the car is fitted with belts wear them in the interests of safety, otherwise you may run the risk of a police fine.

Signals

Signals of a driver's intentions must be clearly given, within a reasonable distance and in good time. In built-up areas, the general rule is not to use the horn unless safety demands it. In many large towns and resorts, as well as in areas indicated by the international sign, the use of the horn is totally prohibited.

Speed limits

It is important to observe the speed limits at all times. Offenders may be fined and driving licences confiscated on the spot, causing great inconvenience and possibly expense. The limits may be varied by road signs and where such signs are displayed the lower limit should be accepted. At certain times limits may also be temporarily varied and information should be available at the frontier. It can be an offence to travel at so slow a speed as to obstruct the traffic flow without good reason, but remember that if you have not held a full licence (not provisional) for one year your top speed is restricted to 90kph (56mph) in France and Portugal.

Traffic lights

In principle city and town traffic lights operate in a way similar to those in the United Kingdom, although they are sometimes suspended overhead. The density of the light may be so poor that the lights may be missed. There is usually only one set on the right-hand side of the road some distance before the road junction, and if you stop too close to the corner the lights will not be visible. Watch out for filter lights which enable vehicles to turn right at a junction against the main lights. Cars wishing to go straight ahead should not enter a lane leading to a filter light otherwise they may obstruct traffic wishing to turn right.

Trams

Trams take priority over other vehicles. Always give way to passengers boarding and alighting. Never position a vehicle so that it impedes the free passage of a tram. Trams must be overtaken on the right, except in one-way streets.

Warning triangles

A warning triangle is compulsory when driving almost anywhere on the continent. The two countries where the use of a warning triangle is recommended rather than compulsory are Sweden and Yugoslavia. The triangle has to be put about 0.6 m (2 ft) from the edge of the road, when a vehicle has broken down, and about 30 m (33 yd) behind the vehicle. On motorways this distance is increased to 100 m (110 yd).

CAMP-SITE COSTS IN EUROPE

It is difficult to give an average cost per night. So much depends on whether the site is privately owned or run by the local authority, by the sea or inland and what facilities are available. As a very rough guide £5 a night per family or 'unit' right across Europe seems reasonable. This can go down to £3 on a small inland site and rise to as much as £10 per night on a high-rating site in a popular seaside resort.

FRANCE

The country

It is not surprising that France, Europe's largest country, is the number-one choice with British campers. It has a climate and a terrain more varied than any other western European country, a historic past to equal our own, and infinitely more space than we have.

Camping is very well organized in France. There have been two major alterations in the system in the past thirty years. Today there are some 6,800 officially graded sites in the country. Grades are denoted by stars, a top-grade four-star site having comprehensive amenities, landscaped grounds, an emphasis on comfort and no over-crowding. A three-star site has first-class amenities, a two-star site good all-round standards, while on a one-star site the amenities are basic. Over a third of official sites fall into the three- or four-star categories.

Prices are fixed annually by the relevant local authorities, each district deciding its own price structure, but three- and four-star sites may fix their own charges above those laid down by the authorities. Some of the three- and four-star sites charge by the unit, others per person, with the tent, the car and the pitch *(emplacement)* all counting as separate items. There is generally a lower rate for children. Charges, as with most countries, are per day and usually run from midday to midday. To guard against overcharging, a government regulation lays down that costs should be displayed near the entrance. In most cases this is done, but sometimes they are inside in reception instead. The star category should be displayed as well.

Since the last reorganization of the camping system in France, there has been a number of improvements and raising of standards. Lavatories and washing cubicles are now usually tiled on three- and four-star sites, and free hot water in showers and dish-washing sinks seem to be becoming more common.

Although over 3,500 sites are commercially run, there are some 2,500 municipal sites in France. These are excellent, and as they are run by local authorities who receive grants towards improving amenities,they often have good toilet facilities and sometimes swimming pools that may be used by the local townspeople. Charges on municipal sites are often lower than those on commercial sites, and while the facilities can vary they are always adequate.

Tourists in France are well catered for by over 5,000 *offices de tourisme* or *syndicats d'initiative* throughout the country. These can supply the names of nearby camp sites as well as information on what to do and see.

There are twenty-two regions in France, each divided into a number of *départements*. Each region has something of its own to offer, but the majority of British families still make for either the Mediterranean or the Atlantic coast. Brittany, which contains a third of the country's coast line, is particularly popular with British campers: it is not too far away, has an excellent selection of camp sites and is not unlike Cornwall but has on the whole a warmer climate. The north coast of the peninsula is cooler and a little more bracing than the south, which can stay warm and sunny well into late September. Brittany is noted for its festivals, its ancient monuments and excellent walks and thus has much more to offer than the typical beach holiday. Many of the rent-a-tent companies have sites in the area.

Normandy, famous for cider and Pont L'Evêque cheese, has some excellent camp sites, some only a short journey from Le

Havre. One of the most agreeable is Colombier, a four-star site at Moyaux near Deauville. Part of the Castels and Camping group, this *château* site has a magnificent swimming pool and the owner, Philippe Charles, provides dinner in the *château* three evenings a week. Canvas Holidays have tents on this suberb site.

Further down the coast Royan is a popular coastal resort, but as this can get quite crowded in the holiday season it may be advisable to camp a little inland and to drive to the coast each day.

The Mediterranean becomes very crowded in the summer, and those who generally never book pitches in other regions of France are advised to make sure of somewhere to stay. They should make reservations if they are using their own gear or, as many people do, use a rent-a-tent company for this part of the country.

The whole of the Mediterranean coast is now developed, the most recent sites appearing at the western end near the Spanish border. Valras Plage seems particularly popular with British campers in this area. It has a fine flat beach and a number of good camp sites. One particularly quiet site a couple of miles outside the very crowded town centre but still close to the coast is Les Foulègues, a three-star site with a modern toilet block. A number of rent-a-tent companies have pitches on another good site nearby, La Yole, which is just a short walk away from the beach, offers plenty of evening entertainment and has a most impressive night guard system.

The Riviera side of the Mediterranean is much more established as a holiday area and therefore has more character and style than the western side, but it is even more crowded.

If you are in search of good beaches, Biarritz in south-west France, with huge Atlantic rollers, is Europe's best and most popular beach for surfing. There are actually three beaches there, with good wide stretches of sand. Two of the most crowded beaches in Europe are in the Riviera, one at Nice and the other at Saint Maxime.

Perhaps the best way to enjoy France is to spend some time at an inland site as well as a seaside one. This is quite easy with your own equipment, and many of the rent-a-tent companies allow campers to change sites: 'site hopping' is, of course, much easier in the low season. One inland site well worth a visit is L'île Offard, on an island in the Loire as it runs through the centre of Saumur. The site, with an official three-star rating, is ideal for exploring the surrounding *châteaux*, and it has a swimming pool – very refreshing after a day's sightseeing. Saumur, famous for its cavalry school, goes back to Roman times and is the centre of one of the oldest wine-growing areas of France. Vouvray, Muscadet and

Anjou wines come from this region. There are well over 100 *châteaux* open to the public along this 275-kilometre (170-mile) stretch of the Loire. Many have *son et lumière* displays and all have some special attraction. The Michelin book *Châteaux of the Loire* (in English) is an excellent guide to take with you, for often the guided tours are in French only.

Lakes make a change from the seaside, and some even have little sandy beaches. The water is often colder than the sea, but a good deal more refreshing than the Mediterranean and the sites less over-camped. For example, an excellent holiday can be had on the quiet shores of Lake Triouzoune near Neuvic d'Ussel in Corrèze, a *département* of Limousin. The lake, close to one of the tributaries of the Dordogne, is good for swimming and children can hire pedal boats. There is a pine forest for walks, a small village for shopping a couple of miles away, and very little else – all adding up to a restful rather than a stimulating break. The site, situated on the edge of the lake, is run by the TCF (the Touring Club de France). It is listed in the AA's *Camping and Caravanning in Europe.* Michelin also lists a municipal site for Neuvic.

A different type of lakeside holiday can be enjoyed at Domaine de Chalain, sited in very agreeable surroundings on the shores of the Chalain lake near the foothills of the Jura and quite close to the Swiss border. It is very efficiently run, has a food take-away, the occasional disco and a television room and library. There is good swimming and boating. Booking is advisable for peak holiday periods.

Last year France's central tourist office improved on a system set up in 1981 for giving campers early warnings on the state of bookings, particularly in popular areas such as the Mediterranean. A leaflet is now produced that people can get before they leave England. Obviously the later you get the leaflet the more up-to-date it is, but do allow four days for delivery. Send a stamped addressed envelope to the French Government Tourist Office (address on page 120). Last year the leaflet listed thirty regional and sixty local information centres which had up-to-date information on the state of bookings in key areas. This year the list could be even longer. Personal callers at the office (no telephone calls are accepted) can get current availability updated daily. The office is open between 9.00 a.m. and 5.00 p.m., Monday to Friday.

If you cannot get hold of the leaflet, look out for tourist information centres along the key touring routes. After the devaluation in 1982 a family with two children and a car were paying between £1.35 on a one-star site and between £5 and £10 on a four-star site in a popular seaside area.

Currency and banking

The unit of currency is the French franc, which is divided into 100 centimes. There is no restriction on the amount of foreign currency which may be taken into France. There is a restriction on taking French money out of the country so check with your bank.

In most large towns banks are open from Monday to Friday from 9.00 a.m. to 4.30 p.m. They close on Saturday and Sunday, and some are also closed on Monday. Banks close at midday on the day prior to a national holiday and all day on Monday if the holiday falls on a Tuesday.

Medical treatment

You must pay for medical and dental treatment and prescribed medicines, but you can get a refund of up to 75 per cent from the French Sickness Insurance Office. You may be asked to pay about 20 per cent of the cost of hospital treatment. The Department of Health and Social Security leaflet SA 36 gives full details.

Public holidays

Holidays based on religious festivals are not always fixed on the calendar and any current diary will give actual dates. The Whit period should not be confused with the British spring bank holiday. Fixed summer holidays are as follows:

1 May	Labour Day
14 July	Bastille Day
15 August	Feast of the Assumption

Shopping hours

Department stores are usually open from Monday to Saturday from 10.00 a.m. to 1.00 p.m. and from 3.00 to 7.00 p.m., although food shops open at 8.30 a.m. and may also open on Sunday mornings.

Motoring information

If you require any of the accident services, contact the police *(brigade de gendarmerie)*, particularly in cases of injury. Emergency telephone boxes are stationed every 20 km (12 miles) on some roads and are connected direct to the local police station. In the larger towns emergency help can be obtained from the emergency assistance department *(police secours)*.

Motorists involved in a traffic accident must complete a *constat à l'amiable*, a European accident statement form, before the vehicle is moved. If the vehicle has been seriously damaged an expert's examination is advised prior to the return to the UK.

Breakdowns

If your car breaks down, try to move it to the verge of the road so that it obstructs the traffic flow as little as possible. Place a warning triangle behind it to warn following traffic. On most of the major routes, at intervals of 3 or 5 kilometres (2 or 3 miles), signs that say Touring Club de France, Secours Automobile, *poste d'appel en cas d'urgence*, outside shops, cafes, etc., indicate that a telephone call may be made from there to the nearest garage providing breakdown service. The police will also help by calling assistance.

Drinking and driving

A driver with more than the permitted level of alcohol in his or her blood is considered to be under the influence of alcohol and is therefore subject to a penalty.

Lights

Headlights should be adapted so that they dip to the right. Motorists are advised to comply with the French law which requires all vehicles to be equipped with headlights with a yellow beam. It is obligatory to use headlights as driving on side-lights only is not permitted. In fog, mist, or poor visibility during the day or night, either two foglights or two dipped headlights must be switched on in addition to two sidelights. Failure to comply with this regulation will lead to a fine. Parking lights must be used in badly lit areas and when visibility is poor.

Priority

Motorists should be extra careful when driving in France. In built-up areas, drivers must slow down and be prepared to stop at all road junctions. In the past couple of years new regulations and signs for priority have been enforced. If there is no priority sign (a blue arrow on a yellow triangle) give way to traffic from the right, but you have priority on roads bearing the sign *'Passage protégé'*. Secondary roads are marked with a 'stop' sign or a yellow triangle with a red border. On steep gradients, vehicles travelling downhill must give way to vehicles travelling uphill. Always give way to street-cleaning vehicles.

Road conditions

France has an excellent and comprehensive network of roads, the surfaces of which are normally good; exceptions are usually signposted *'chaussée deformée'*. When this occurs the camber is often severe and the edges rough. There is a countrywide network of routes nationales for those who do not wish to use the tollways. The D roads (D stands for department and not an inferior type of road) are often excellent. For those who do use the tollways, the stopping places (aires) are so good as to make up somewhat for the expense of travelling on these motorways. They contain shops and restaurants and most have beautifully clean toilet facilities.

Holiday traffic

During July and August, and especially at weekends, traffic on the main roads is likely to be very heavy. Special signs are erected to indicate routes with the least traffic congestion. Wherever they appear it is usually worth following them. Green arrows on a white background are used to indicate alternative routes *(itinéraires bis)* to congested main roads in a north–south direction. A white arrow on a green background indicates an alternative in a south–north direction. Yellow arrows on a blue background indicate alternative routes *(itinéraires de délestage)* by-passing busy towns. Signs are posted at regular intervals throughout the alternatives.

Seat belts
If your vehicle is fitted with seat belts, it is compulsory to wear them.

GERMANY

The country
Over the past few years Germany has become more popular with British holidaymakers, and deservedly so, for it has plenty to offer. Germany has a temperate climate, which means from the holidaymaker's point of view that the nights are cool enough for comfortable sleep, and although the weather can be variable it is on the whole hotter during the summer than in Great Britain.

There are well over 2,000 camp sites in the country, some 400 of which have been selected for the list issued by the German Tourist Office. German camp sites are generally well run, with well built toilet blocks and clean pitches. A plus point is that the majority of the sites have a swimming pool, however small.

The camping season runs from May to September, with many sites staying open throughout the year. A number of these heat their washrooms during the cool weather, and hot water is usually free at all times.

Camping is very popular in Germany, so good sites in popular areas tend to get crowded by the Germans themselves, especially in July. Although the *Happy Days in Germany* brochure, issued by the German tourist office, claims that reservations are not generally made, both Alan Rogers and the AA recommend it.

There are a number of municipal sites in Germany and these are listed in the local town brochure. The network catering for tourists in Germany is good – most towns and villages have a tourist office, where information can be obtained, usually near the station or the town hall. As with any country, there will be badly run sites, but these are less common in Germany than in southern Europe.

As to where to go, the northern part of the country, including Schleswig-Holstein, Lower Saxony, Hamburg and Bremen, is not as well known to British visitors as the south, probably because it is less accessible. Europe's fourth largest port and Germany's second city, Hamburg, is over 640 kilometres (400 miles) from Ostend, although there is a direct, though long, sea crossing to Hamburg from Harwich. There are enchanting medieval towns in this part of the country, wooded hills and lakes. The Plon Lakes are good for boating but are very popular with German campers in July, as are the camp sites on the Baltic coast.

Central Germany is well wooded with pine and beech forests, where it is not broken up by the industrial areas in Westphalia between the Ruhr and the Lippe rivers. This part of the country officially includes the Rhineland, Westphalia, Hesse, the Rhineland-Palatinate and the Saarland. The Rhineland is very popular and camps there can be crowded in summer.

However, the beautiful Moselle river, also in central Germany, is in an equally attractive area, famous for its vineyards and well worth a visit. The town of Winningen, in the biggest wine-growing area of the Moselle, holds Germany's oldest wine festival in the last week of August. This part of Germany, close to Belgium, Luxembourg and France, is easier to reach than you might suppose: Trier, on the Moselle and in the heart of the Moselle-Saar-Ruwer wine-making region, is only about 320 kilometres (200 miles) from Ostend, a drive through very agreeable Belgian countryside, including the Ardennes. Trier is also interesting from a historic point of view – it is Germany's oldest city and was the second city of the Roman Empire. Its classic ruins, which include an amphitheatre, baths and the famous Porta Nigra, are in better condition than many of the monuments in Rome itself. There is an excellent tourist office. Trier has two camp sites: one in the town, the other just outside on the banks of the Moselle which makes a quieter base for touring. There are plenty of camp sites in the Moselle area but not all that many on the river's edge. A particularly attractive one, Campingplatz Burgen, lies between Koblenz and Cochem.

Probably southern Germany – Bavaria and the Black Forest – is better known to English holidaymakers. The Bavarian National Forest, Germany's first national park, has a number of well-equipped sites in areas of outstanding natural beauty. It is in southern Germany that there is so much emphasis on the romantic aspect of the landscape and the buildings, with scenic routes having such names as the Idyllic Road, the Romantic Road, the Siegfried Road, and so on. The Black Forest area is becoming popular with rent-a-tent companies, generally a sign that the camp sites are good.

How to get there
If you use one of the short-crossing Channel ferries and travel via Belgium, West Germany is just within a day's drive. The distance

from Calais to Cologne is just under 410 kilometres (260 miles). If you drive through northern France and enter Germany near Strasbourg, the journey usually takes two days. This entry point is also used if travelling by the longer Channel crossings: Cherbourg, Dieppe, or Le Havre are best for southern Germany. The distance from Le Havre to Strasbourg is just under 688 kilometres (430 miles), a journey which will take one to two days.

For visiting northern Germany ferries operating across the North Sea to the Netherlands can be an advantage. Alternatively, it is possible to use the ferries operating between Harwich and Bremerhaven or Hamburg.

Currency and banking

The unit of currency is the Deutschmark, which is divided into 100 Pfennig. Sterling traveller's cheques can be exchanged at all banks, savings banks, exchange offices at frontiers, main railway stations and airports. There is no limit to the sum of money which may be imported or exported, either in German or in foreign currency.

Most banks are open from Monday to Wednesday and on Friday from 8.30 to 12.00 a.m. and from 2.00 to 3.30 p.m. On Thursday the morning opening hours are similar, but afternoon hours are 2.00 to 5.30. The banks are closed on Saturdays. Exchange offices of the Deutsche-Verkehrs-Kredit-Bank are located at main railway stations, and road and rail frontier crossing points. Generally these are open from early morning until late at night.

Medical treatment

Hospital, other medical and dental treatment is free. You may have to pay a small charge for prescribed medicine. The Department of Health and Social Security leaflet SA 36 gives full details.

Public holidays

Holidays based on religious festivals are not always fixed on the calendar but any current diary will give actual dates. The Whit period (a religious holiday) should not be confused with the British spring bank holiday. Fixed summer holidays are as follows:

1 May	Labour Day
17 June	National Day
15 August	Feast of the Assumption

Shopping hours

Food shops are generally open from Monday to Friday from 7.00 a.m. to 1.00 p.m. and from 2.00 to 6.00 p.m.; Saturday hours are 7.00 a.m. to 1.00 p.m. Department stores open from Monday to Friday from 9.00 a.m. to 6.30 p.m., some closing for lunch between 1.00 and 3.00 p.m. On Saturdays they are open from 9.00 a.m. to 2.00 p.m.

Motoring accidents

You are generally required to call the police when individuals have been injured or considerable damage has been caused. Not to give aid to anyone injured will render you liable to a fine.

Breakdowns

If your car breaks down, try to move it to the verge of the road so that it does not obstruct traffic flow. A warning triangle must be placed behind the car and hazard warning lights, if fitted, must be used. The German motoring organization, (the ADAC) operates a breakdown service (the Strassenwacht) similar to that run by the AA. Patrol cars operate on motorways, on the more important roads and in urban areas. On motorways, patrols are notified by the Motorway Authorities whom you contact by using the emergency telephones. The direction of the nearest telephone is indicated by the point of the black triangle on posts alongside the motorways.

Drinking and driving

If there is a definite suspicion that a driver is under the influence of alcohol, the police can compel him or her to undergo a blood test. However, no one can be made to undergo a breath test (breathalyser). A convicted driver is always punished by imprisonment, fine and/or suspension of driving licence. A visiting motorist who is convicted will not be allowed to drive in Germany, and this will be noted on his/her driving licence.

Parking

Spending the night in a vehicle is tolerated providing that there are no signs forbidding it and that the vehicle is lit and parked in a lay-by. The sign showing an eagle in a green triangle (wildlife reserve) prohibits parking outside parking lots.

Priority

On pedestrian (zebra) crossings pedestrians have the right of way over all vehicles except trams. Buses have priority when leaving public bus stops and other vehicles must give way to a bus driver who has signalled his intention to leave the kerb.

Road conditions

The *Bundestrassen* (state roads) vary in quality. In the north and in the touring areas of the Rhine Valley, Black Forest and Bavaria, the roads are good and well graded. The *Autobahnen* (motorways) are excellent and there are no tolls.

Holiday traffic

Traffic at weekends increases considerably during the school holidays which are from July to mid-September. In order to ease congestion, heavy lorries are prohibited on all roads at weekends from approximately mid-June to the end of August and generally on all Sundays and public holidays.

SPAIN
The country

For years Spain has been popular with British holidaymakers, campers as well as those on package holidays. For thousands of people the country, the second largest in western Europe, conjures up a mental picture of reliable sunshine, miles of excellent beaches and cheap food and drink. The sunshine and beaches are still there but democracy has caused prices to rise considerably over the past few years.

The climate, temperate in the north, hot and dry in the south, tempts many campers to make the formidable drive – some 1,600 kilometres (1,000 miles) – from the French Channel ports to the Spanish Mediterranean. For those unwilling to attempt such a marathon, Brittany Ferries, the only company to offer a car ferry service direct to Spain, has a twice-weekly crossing from Plymouth to Santander. This takes twenty-four hours and cost £512 return for a family of four with a cabin in the 1982 high season; in the first half of July the return fare cost £420.

Most of the six hundred or so camp sites in Spain are on the coast, particularly on the 1,120 kilometres (700 miles) of the Mediterranean coast. Much of the great central plateau of Spain, mountainous and barren, is just not suitable for camping. There are a number of sites round Madrid, right in the centre of the country, a good few in the north of the country just below the Pyrenees, and a reasonable selection on the Atlantic coast. Sites are officially classified according to the facilities and services they offer, and the site classification, one to three with a special luxury class, should be displayed on a board near the entrance. Sites vary enormously from the really appalling to the superbly luxurious. Some of these *campings de lujo* have everything from dance floors to hairdressing salons and are beautifully laid out with trees, flowers and shrubs.

Tourism is important to Spain and strenuous efforts have been made over the past years to improve the standard of some of the sites. However good the facilities though, there is not the organization that exists in French or German sites. Pitches may be marked out, but often the amount of ground per tent is small and generally you are left to find your own pitch. When the pressure is on in the high season, some site proprietors are inclined to ignore pitch markings and let the site get overcrowded. The 'silence after 11.00 p.m.' rule does not exist in Spain – in fact the night is often just beginning then. Because of the midday heat and the long siesta, Spanish meals run much later than in the rest of Europe so the whole day is displaced. Some sites, however, are beginning to ask that a silence rule be observed between 11.00 p.m. and 8.00 a.m.

The long Mediterranean coastline of Spain has five 'costas', stretching from the French border to the southern tip of the country. Alicante on the Costa del Sol, is said to be one of the hottest places in the country between July and August, so southern Spain is not the place to take young children camping during high summer. The Costa Brava (where there are more camp sites along the excellent beaches and somewhat inland than there are in the whole of the rest of Spain) is the most popular Costa with British campers. Castell Montgri, in Gerona just outside Estartit on the Costa Brava, is said to be a well run site with excellent facilities.

We have stayed at a very good site on the Costa Dorada. Just eight kilometres (five miles) north of Tarragona the site, Torre de la Mora, in the first classification of the Spanish tourist office list, is just above the beach, has shady marked-out pitches and was reasonably quiet when we were there.

Some of the camps on the Mediterranean coast, particularly those close to Barcelona are gigantic, often catering for up to 5,000 people. Generally, the closer a camp is to a town the noisier it is.

The sites along the Atlantic coast are not as popular. Possibly because this ocean is colder than the Mediterranean and the weather not so reliable. But the countryside is magnificent and the sites tend to be smaller than those on the Mediterranean coast. I have heard good reports of a site some 288 kilometres (180 miles) from Santander. Camping los Cantiles, 3 kilometres (2 miles) from Luarca, is said to have a good atmosphere and immaculately clean toilets, although no hot water is available during the summer. There is no organised entertainment on the camp sites on this coast; the sangria parties and barbecues are much more a feature of the Mediterranean sites.

There are some good sites in northern Spain. We found an excellent one when driving from the Atlantic to the Mediterranean: Camping Pirineos at Santa Cilia de Jaca had a marvellous swimming pool and plenty of shade.

Much of the ground in Spain is hard and rocky, so steel tent pegs as well as large wooden ones should be included in the kits of those taking their own camping gear. The wooden pegs are for the soft sandy ground often found on seaside sites. Extra plastic sheeting put under the inner tents will help prevent the floors being damaged by rough ground.

How to get there

From the Channel ports Spain is approached via France. The two main routes are at either end of the Pyrenees: the Biarritz to San Sebastian road, or motorway, at the western end for central and southern Spain, and the Perpignan to Barcelona road, or motorway, at the eastern end for the Costa Brava.

Currency and banking

The unit of currency is the peseta, which is divided into 100 centimos. There are no restrictions on importing or exporting foreign currencies or traveller's cheques if a declaration is made to the customs on entry. Traveller's cheques may be changed only at banks, authorized travel agencies or hotels.

Banks are usually open from 9.00 a.m. to 2.00 p.m., Monday to Saturday. There are exchange offices at travel agents which are open from 9.00 a.m. to 1.00 p.m. and 4.00 to 7.00 p.m. Monday to Friday, and from 9.00 a.m. to 1.00 p.m. on Saturday.

Medical treatment

There is no free medical treatment for visitors and it is advisable to have adequate insurance for this.

Public holidays

Holidays based on religious festivals are not always fixed on the calendar but any current diary will give actual dates. The Whit period (a religious holiday) should not be confused with the British spring bank holiday. Fixed summer holidays are as follows:

19 March	St Joseph's Day
1 May	St Joseph the Worker
15 May	Madrid only
25 July	St James of Spain
15 August	Feast of the Assumption
12 October	Our Lady of El Pilar

Shopping hours

Food shops are open Monday to Saturday from 9.00 a.m. to 1.00/1.30 p.m. and from 3.00/3.30 to 7.30/8.00 p.m. Other stores' hours are 10.00 a.m. to 8.00 p.m., though some close earlier.

Motoring information and regulations

There is an assistance service for the victims of traffic accidents which is run by the Central Traffic Department. At present this ambulance service, which operates day and night, is available only on certain roads. Get precise details from either the Spanish National Tourist Office or the AA's *Travellers' Guide in Europe.* There is an SOS telephone network on the roads where this service operates. Motorists in need of help should ask for road assistance *(auxilio en carretera).* The special ambulances used are in radio contact with the hospital taking part in the scheme.

Breakdowns

If your car breaks down, try to move it to the verge of the road so that it obstructs the traffic as little as possible, and place a warning triangle behind it. A twenty-four-hour breakdown service is run by the Spanish Motoring Club (RACE) in the Madrid area only and is available to touring motorists. To obtain assistance telephone Madrid 7543344. Elsewhere in Spain there is no road-patrol service, and if you need help you must make your own arrangements with a garage.

Driving licence

A British driving licence is acceptable in Spain but only if accompanied by an official translation stamped by a Spanish consulate. It is recommended that you carry an International Driving Permit which costs less than the official stamping and translation.

Bail bond

An accident in Spain can have very serious consequences, including the impounding of the car and property, and the detention of the driver pending bail. A bail bond can often facilitate the release of person and property, and you are advised to obtain one of these from your insurer, for a nominal premium, when you get your green card. A bail bond is a written guarantee that a cash deposit of usually up to £1,500 will be paid to the Spanish Court as surety for bail, and as security for any fine which may be imposed, although in such an event you will have to reimburse any amounts paid by your insurers.

Drinking and driving

A driver suspected of driving while under the influence of alcohol may be asked to undergo a breath test. A heavy fine, together with the withdrawal of the driving licence, will be imposed on a person found guilty.

Road conditions

There are about 1,930 kilometres (1,200 miles) of motorway *(autopista)* open in Spain with more under construction. Apart from a few stretches of toll-free motorway near Barcelona and Madrid, tolls are charged. The surface of the main roads varies, but on the whole is good; traffic is light. The roads are winding in many places, and at times it is not advisable to exceed 48-56 kph (30-35 mph). Secondary roads, seldom numbered, are often rough, winding and encumbered by slow horse-drawn traffic.

Road signs

All main roads prefixed 'N', six of those radiating from Madrid, are numbered in Roman numerals. Secondary roads are prefixed 'C'.

Holiday traffic

Holiday traffic, particularly on the coast road to Barcelona and Tarragona and in the San Sebastian area, causes congestion which may be severe at weekends.

ITALY

The country

Italy is at least a 1,130 kilometre (700 mile) drive from the French Channel ports, while the journey to Rome is over 1,600 kilometres (1,000 miles). Partly because of the distance, but also because of the extreme heat of southern Italy, most English families go no further south than Florence when camping, although central Italy is very beautiful.

Camping has grown in popularity in Italy over the past fifteen years, with the Italians themselves, never previously very keen on living in tents, recently taking to it *en famille*. Sites, already full with other European visitors, tend to get very overcrowded during the first three weeks of August when many Italian factories close for the summer holiday.

The Italian Camping Federation, whose headquarters are in Florence, began in 1950, and most of the 1,600 sites in the country, both privately run or managed by organizations, are connected with the Federation. Once site standards have been approved, proprietors are granted a licence through the provincial tourist office. This licence can be withdrawn if standards fall. The regulations state that sites must provide, among other requirements, adequate sanitary facilities, a secure enclosure and guarding and lighting on the site at night. It is said that security is not always as well enforced as it is on some French sites, so it is particularly important to take out insurance against theft when camping in Italy.

No grading system is used to classify sites, and campers therefore have to base their decision on where to stay on the list of facilities. In such a situation the personal comments in a guide book such as that by Alan Rogers (see page 74) are helpful. So too are reports in camping magazines and the comments of friends who have already camped in Italy.

Top sites are similar to those all over Europe, and the fact that a number of reputable rent-a-tent companies are now offering holidays on Italian sites indicates that a number have excellent facilities. It is said that a site at Cecina, Camping Montescudigo, set in a forest, is superbly equipped. A few years ago *Trail* magazine gave top marks to Camping del Sole, a site at Iseo in Brescia off the A3 *autostrada* between Milan and Venice. A camp site on the Tuscany coast, Camping Cicloverde, about 95 kilometres (58 miles) from the medieval town of Sienna, is one of the best sites in Italy, if not in Europe. Although it was opened only a couple of years ago, it is on a mature site superbly set in 60 hectares (150 acres) of well established woodland where many of the tall pines are well over a century old. The site, which can take up to 1,000 tents, has scrupulously clean toilet blocks and a well equipped shop that sells a wide selection of goods at moderate prices, and is about a mile from the beach. 'Airport' buses in the camp colours of blue and green run a constant service between site and sea. Great pots of exotic plants adorn the site, sprinklers keep the grass brilliantly green and such attention is paid to cleanliness that each tent holder is given a free ration of plastic rubbish bags. The computerized office, backed by a sick bay with attendant nurse and visiting doctor and the generous size of pitches (a good 100 sq m, 110 sq yd) put this site well in the top category. A family of four with their own gear could expect to pay around £10 a night, inclusive of hot water. One English operator, Inn-Tent, has fifteen tents ready erected at Cicloverde.

The camping season stretches from May until the end of August, the period from mid-July to mid-August inevitably being the most popular. It is best to book if you plan a seaside or lake-based holiday during this time. In 1982 Italy re-introduced petrol discount coupons, free motorway toll vouchers and free breakdown service. The coupons are available to personal callers only at AA offices and port centres. You will need passport and vehicle registration document.

How to get there

Although there are several ways of getting to Italy, you will probably enter via France or Switzerland. The major passes, which are closed in winter, are served by road or rail tunnels. Motorail and car-sleeper services operate during the summer from Boulogne, Brussels and Paris to Milan.

Currency and banking

The unit of currency is the lira. There are certain restrictions on the importing of Italian bank notes but there is no import restriction on other currencies.

Banking hours are generally 8.30 a.m. to 1.30 p.m., Monday to Friday.

Medical treatment

Hospital, other medical and dental treatment is free. However, a small charge is made for some prescribed medicines. The Department of Health and Social Security leaflet SA36 gives full details.

Public holidays

Holidays based on religious festivals are not always fixed on the calendar but any current diary will give the actual dates. The Whit holiday should not be confused with the British spring bank holiday. Fixed summer holidays are as follows:

153

<pre>
        25 April   Liberation Day
        1 May   Labour Day
        15 August   Feast of the Assumption
</pre>

Shopping hours

Most shops are usually open from Monday to Saturday at the following times: food shops from 8.30 a.m. to 1.00 p.m. and 4.00 to 8.00 p.m.; other shops from 9.00 a.m. to 1.00 p.m. and 4.00 to 7.30 p.m.

All shops close on Saturday afternoon during the summer.

Motoring accidents

No particular procedure is required following an accident, excepting that a report must be made to the insurance company within three days. If the accident involves personal injury, it is obligatory that medical assistance is sought for the injured party, and that the incident is reported to the police. On some *autostrade* (motorways) there are emergency telephones as well as emergency push-button call boxes.

Breakdowns

Try to move the car to the verge of the road, and place a warning triangle behind it.

The Soccorso Stradale Gratuito ACI (Soccorso Autostradale SAS on motorways) is a breakdown service operated by the Automobile Club d'Italia (ACI). This twenty-four-hour seven-day-a-week service, which is not available for caravans, can be reached by dialling 116 from public telephone boxes. Emergency telephones on motorways may also be used. All services must be paid for and a calling fee will also be levied.

Drinking and driving

Any driver found to be driving under the influence of alcohol may be sentenced to a term of imprisonment of up to six months and fined.

Using the horn

In built-up areas the use of the horn is prohibited except in cases of immediate danger. At night flashing headlights may be used instead of the horn. Outside built-up areas it is compulsory to use the horn when warning of approach is necessary.

Lights

Full-beam headlights can be used only outside cities and towns. Dipped headlights are compulsory when passing through tunnels and bridges even if they are well lit.

Priority

Traffic on state highways *(strada statali)*, which are all numbered and indicated by signs, has right of way, as do public service vehicles and postal buses. These postal bus routes are indicated by a special sign.

154

If two vehicles are travelling in opposite directions and the drivers of each want to turn left they must pass in front of each other (not drive round as in the UK).

Road conditions

There are almost 6,450 kilometres (4,000 miles) of motorway on which tolls are levied. Main roads are generally in good condition, but secondary roads are often poor. Coastal roads are very busy in the summer.

BELGIUM

The country

As Belgium's reputation for being expensive fades away more British families are camping in this delightful little country which has a passion for historical pageants. Belgium is under four hours' crossing from Dover to Ostend by motor vessel and only 1½ hours by jetfoil. There is a fair amount of industry in the north of the country, but there are wide and safe sandy beaches on the Ostend coast and the lovely countryside of the Ardennes is less than a day's drive from the ports. Flemish and French are the main languages, with a small minority of people in the east of the country speaking German. English is widely spoken, particularly in shops, restaurants and camp sites.

Belgium has reorganized its whole camping structure over the past decade and now has over five hundred sites classified into one of four categories. The free leaflet issued by the Belgian tourist office lists three hundred of these licensed sites, and explains the requirements of each of the four categories. A new site is automatically put into the one-star category when the owner applies for a licence, so do not dismiss these low-graded sites too lightly. Often, too, a proprietor has made the necessary improvements to move his site up a couple of categories but has not yet been awarded more stars. So it is always worth inspecting one- or two-star sites – you may end up by paying lower prices for three- or four-star facilities.

The Belgians, like the French and Germans, are fond of camping, and therefore sites, particularly round the coast, tend to get very crowded. Camps are generally open from April till October, with a number staying open throughout the year.

How to get there

Many cross-Channel ferries operate direct from Dover and Folkestone to Ostend, or from Dover, Felixstowe and Hull to Zeebrugge. Alternatively, it is possible to use the shorter Channel crossings from Dover or Folkestone to France and drive along the coastal road to Belgium. Fast hovercraft services operate from Dover or Ramsgate to Calais and from Dover to Boulogne.

Remember that the jetfoil service from Dover to Ostend is quick, but does not take vehicles.

Currency and banking

The unit of currency is the Belgian franc, divided into 100 centimes. There is no restriction on the amount of currency which may be taken into or out of the country. As Belgian currency regulations are subject to change, intending visitors should familiarize themselves with the current exchange regulations before leaving Britain.

Banks are generally open from 9.00 a.m. to 3.30 p.m. from Monday to Friday, and are closed all day Saturday. Many also close for lunch. Outside banking hours currency can be exchanged in Brussels at the Gare du Nord and the Gare du Midi, from 6.00 a.m. to 10.00 p.m. daily.

Public holidays

Holidays based on religious festivals are not always fixed on the calendar but any current diary will give the actual dates. The Whit holiday should not be confused with the British spring bank holiday. Fixed summer holidays are as follows:

1 May Labour Day
21 July National holiday
15 August Feast of the Assumption

Shopping hours

All shops are usually open 9.00 a.m. to 6.00 or 7.00 p.m. from Monday to Saturday. Food shops, however, may close one hour later.

Motoring accidents

Where damage to vehicles only has occurred, vehicles must be removed after the drivers have exchanged particulars. The police must be called if an unoccupied stationary vehicle is damaged or if injuries are caused to persons; in the latter case the car must not be moved.

Breakdowns

The Belgian Motoring Club (TCB) maintains an efficient breakdown service known as Touring Secours/Touring Wegenhulp.

Drinking and Driving

A driver with more than the permitted level of alcohol in his or her blood may be punished by a fine and/or a prison sentence of between fifteen days and six months; in addition the driver may be disqualified.

Road conditions

On the whole road conditions are good. Free motorways serve most of the country.

Road signs
The international route that has given more cause for complaint than any other is that from Calais to Cologne in Germany which passes through Belgium. The problem is aggravated firstly by the existence of two official languages in Belgium, and secondly by the fact that in the Flemish part of Belgium all signs are in Flemish only, while in the French part of the country the signs are all in French. Brussels seems to be the only neutral ground where signs show the two spellings of place-names (Antwerpen – Anvers; Gent – Gand; Liège – Luik) and so on.

LUXEMBOURG
The country
The tiny Grand Duchy of Luxembourg, only 2,500 square kilometres (1,560 square miles), is flanked by Belgium, France and Germany. It is a country with much scenic variety and plenty of forests, the best known being the Ardennes, close to Belgium, in the north. Luxembourg is good walking country with the network of footpaths probably being the densest in Europe. French and German are the official languages with English being understood in many places.

Luxembourg has a temperate climate with most of the tourist areas being well sheltered from cold winds. Most of the 100 or so official camp sites are open from April till October. July and August are the most crowded months although June and September are said to be sunnier. Camp-site control is taken seriously and is watched over by a Minister of Tourism; sites can be closed if they do not keep standards up. There are four categories of site with the third class offering the fewest facilities. A definition of what each category provides is given in the list of sites put out by the tourist office. It is worth noting that a 'pilote' site is not, as might sound, a new site, but one in the luxury class offering more than a first class site.

How to get there
The capital city, Luxembourg, is only 320 kilometres (200 miles) from Ostend and about 418 kilometres (260 miles) from Boulogne or Calais and is therefore just a day's drive through either Belgium or France.

Currency and banking
The Luxembourg franc is divided into 100 centimes, and there is no restriction on the amount of local or foreign currency that can be imported or exported. But as there is a limited market for Luxembourg currency in other countries it is wise to change any money before leaving. Belgian money is accepted in Luxembourg. Banks are open from Monday to Friday from 8.00 to 12.00 midday

and from 1.30 p.m. to 4.30 p.m. or 2.00 p.m. to 5.00 p.m. Banks are usually closed on Saturdays.

Medical treatment

Hospital treatment is usually free but you will have to pay for other medical or dental treatment or prescribed medicines. You can get a partial refund from the Luxembourg sickness insurance office. The Department of Health and Social Security leaflet SA36 gives details.

Public holidays

Holidays based on religious festivals are not always fixed on the calendar. The Whit period, a religious holiday, should not be confused with the British spring bank holiday. These are the fixed summer holidays:

1 May	May Day
23 June	National Day
15 August	Feast of the Assumption

Shopping hours

Some shops close on Monday mornings but the usual hours of opening for food shops are from Monday to Saturday 8.00 a.m. to 12.00 midday and 2.00 p.m. to 6.00 p.m. However supermarkets open from 9.00 a.m. to 8.00 p.m. but close at 6.00 p.m. on Saturdays.

Motoring accidents

There are no firm rules to adopt following an accident; however, anyone requested to give assistance must do so.

Breakdowns

The ACL (Automobile Club du Grand-Duché de Luxembourg) operates a 24-hour road assistance service throughout the country. ACL vehicles are yellow and have 'Automobile Club Service Routier' on them. The Secours Automobile Luxembourg is a commercial breakdown concern which does not accept the credit vouchers included in some insurance packages.

Drinking and driving

Anyone suspected of driving while under the influence of alcohol may have to undergo a breath test. If convicted a driver faces severe penalties including fines and/or imprisonment.

Road conditions

Luxembourg has a comprehensive system of good main and secondary roads.

THE NETHERLANDS

The country

The Netherlands can be very enjoyable. The climate is mild, with moderate rather than hot summers. There are 120 kilometres (80 miles) or so of beaches along the North Sea coast which boasts over fifty resorts. Scheveningen, famous at the turn of the century as a seaside town, is making strenuous efforts to return to its former glory though this time, with an eye to modern tastes, it is installing sports complexes and providing plenty of entertainment for days when the weather is not so good.

There is an excellent tourist structure in the Netherlands and the tourist offices, distinguished by their VVV signs, are able to provide information on camp sites as well as what to do and see. The country has over 2,000 camp sites as the Dutch themselves are very keen campers. There is no official grading system, but some 350 camps have been included in the official camping brochure issued by the tourist office. The Dutch holiday period extends from mid-July to mid-August, during which time sites are crowded, but there is an efficient booking service.

How to get there
There are direct ferry services to the Netherlands. Services operate from Harwich to the Hook of Holland, Hull to Rotterdam, Felixstowe to Rotterdam, and Sheerness to Flushing. The sea journey can take between seven and fourteen hours, depending on the port of departure. Alternatively, use one of the short Channel crossings and complete the journey by driving through France and Belgium. The distance from Calais to Den Haag is just under 352 kilometres (220 miles) and is within a day's drive.

Currency and banking
The unit of currency is the gulden (Fl), also known as the guilder, which is divided into 100 cents. There are no restrictions on the import or export of currency.

Medical treatment
Hospital and other medical treatment and prescribed medicines are free but you may have to pay part of the cost of dental treatment. The Department of Health and Social Security leaflet SA36 gives full details.

Public holidays
Holidays based on religious festivals such as Good Friday and Ascension Day are not always fixed on the calendar, but any current diary will give the actual dates. The Whit period should not be confused with the British spring bank holiday. There are no fixed summer holidays in the Netherlands.

Shopping hours
Stores are open on Mondays from 1.00 to 6.00 p.m. and on Tuesdays to Saturdays from 9.00 a.m. to 6.00 p.m. (5.00 on Saturdays). Food shops are open from 8.30 a.m. to 6.00 p.m. (5.00 on Saturdays).

Motoring accidents

In the event of a serious or complicated accident, especially when personal injury has been sustained, the police should be called before the vehicle is removed.

Breakdowns

If the car breaks down, try to move it to the verge of the road and place a warning triangle behind it.

Drinking and driving

Drivers suspected of having drunk alcohol may be required to undergo a blood test. Penalties for those found guilty of driving under the influence of alcohol include a term of imprisonment and a driving ban of up to five years.

Priority

Regulations in the Netherlands take into account the very large numbers of cyclists for whom special tracks are provided on a number of roads. Motor vehicles generally have priority over this slower-moving traffic except when controlled by the appropriate road signs. However, cyclists proceeding straight ahead at intersections have priority over all turning traffic: visitors should be particularly alert to this rule.

Road conditions

Main roads usually have only two lanes but are well surfaced. The best way to see the countryside is to tour along minor roads, often alongside the canals. There is a network of motorways *(autosnelweg)* carrying most inter-city and long-distance traffic.

DENMARK

The country

Denmark, which shares a border with Germany, is a land of small lakes, fjords and islands – some five hundred of them. It has few rivers or mountains but a coastline over 8,000 kilometres (5,000 miles) long and good beaches everywhere. The climate is mild and the summer lasts from June until the end of August. The weather can be changeable but there are long, warm, dry periods. During the summer the nights are short and light, but often chilly. Danish is the national language but English is readily understood and is the second language.

Danish camp sites, both those run by private enterprise and by local authorities, are generally good and a close watch is kept on standards, with official sites receiving regular visits from health inspectors. Sites are officially classified by a star system, with one-star sites fulfilling the minimum requirements and some three-star sites even boasting saunas. There are over 500 sites that have been approved and classified by the National Camping Committee. Sites that have been approved by camp inspectors display a green wigwam sign and the words *'godkent lejrplads'* which means 'approved camp site'.

There is no set procedure for booking on a Danish site. Some accept advance bookings while others, such as the large Absalon site at Copenhagen, operate purely on a first come, first served basis. Denmark is one of the few European countries to insist on a camping carnet being produced before a pitch can be used. Campers without one can buy a temporary permit from the site warden. Sites are open from May to September with about 100 remaining open throughout the year. Most sites close at 10.00 p.m. and the no-noise rule is usually observed. Because Denmark has an extensive coastline many sites are not too far from the sea.

How to get there

The two main ways of reaching Denmark are by using the direct ferry services from Newcastle or Harwich to Esbjerg in western Jutland, or by using one of the short Channel crossings to France or Belgium and completing the journey by road through the Netherlands and northern Germany. The distance from the Channel ports to Copenhagen is roughly 1,060 kilometres (660 miles) and the journey would require one or two overnight stops. Another possibility is to use the ferries operating between Harwich and Bremerhaven or Hamburg and drive the short distance to southern Denmark. Inter-island travel is made easy by either bridge links or frequent vehicle ferries.

Currency and banking

The unit of currency is the Krone, divided into 100 öre. There is no limit to the amount of foreign or Danish currency which may be imported. However, as there are certain restrictions on the export of Krone ask for advice at your home bank if you plan to take much money out of Denmark on your return.

Banking hours in Copenhagen are from 9.30 a.m. to 4.00 p.m. from Monday to Wednesday and on Friday; on Thursday they are from 9.30 a.m. to noon and from 2.00 to 4.00 p.m. Banks at the Central Railway Station and the Air Terminal are open until 10.00 p.m. Outside Copenhagen usual banking hours are 9.30 a.m. to noon and 2.00 to 4.00 p.m. All banks are closed on Saturday, except the exchange offices on the Danish/German border, which close between 1.00 and 3.00 p.m. These offices may also open on Sunday during the summer.

Medical treatment

UK nationals in need of urgent medical and dental treatment should visit a practitioner who is registered with the Danish Public Health Service. Show your passport and ask for a receipt if you are charged. Approved prescribed medicines can be purchased at a reduced price if you show your passport.

Public holidays

Holidays based on religious festivals are not always fixed on the calendar but any current diary will give actual dates. The Whit period should not be confused with the British spring bank holiday. The fixed summer holiday is:

5 June Constitution Day (midday onwards, but banks closed all day)

Shopping hours

Shops are usually open between 9.00 a.m. and 5.30 p.m. (7.00 or 8.00 p.m. on Friday). Most shops close on Saturday afternoons.

Motoring accidents

If you are involved in a collision or other traffic accident, you must stop and exchange particulars with the other person(s) concerned. If personal injury is sustained, it is obligatory to obtain medical assistance for the injured persons. The incident should then be reported to the police.

Breakdowns

If your car breaks down, try to move it to the verge of the road so that it obstructs the traffic flow as little as possible. The Danish Motoring Club (FDM) is unable to provide roadside assistance. In the event of a breakdown, assistance may be obtained from one of the following organizations which operate a twenty-four-hour service: Road Watch (Vejvagt), FALCK, or the Danish Automobile Assistance Union (Dansk Autojaelp or DAHU).

Drinking and driving

A driver is liable to prosecution if the quantity of alcohol in his blood exceeds 0.80 per cent.

Lights

Left-dipping headlights are prohibited. Headlights should be dipped early when meeting another vehicle as the lighting of Danish-registered vehicles is of lower density than that of UK-registered vehicles. Driving with only one headlight or spotlight is not allowed. Fog lamps may be used in pairs in conjunction with sidelights (but not headlights). In the daytime, when visibility is poor, dipped headlights may be used.

Priority

A line of white triangles painted across the road indicates that you must give way to traffic on the road you are entering.

Road conditions

The roads in Denmark are generally of a very high standard and well signposted.

SWEDEN

The country

With over ten thousand lakes, more than 6,400 kilometres (4,000 miles) of tide-free coastline and millions of acres of forest, Sweden is a country for those fond of the outdoors. Because of the gulf stream it has a temperate climate, the south of the country being warmer than the north. The weather is similar to that in Britain except that there is generally less rain and more sun in June and August and at midsummer it is light for up to nineteen hours a day.

Unfortunately, travelling to Sweden is not cheap. In 1982 in the high season, a family of four paid in the region of £300 to cross the North Sea (this sum included a cabin). Admittedly the direct lines that operate to Sweden are reckoned to have the largest and best-equipped ferries around: there are cinemas, saunas, discos, live music and a swimming pool to while away the twenty-four-hour journey, and the restaurants are said to serve excellent food. For details of camping packages to Scandinavia for those with their own equipment see page 60.

There are about 550 approved camp sites in Sweden, over 70 per cent of which are owned by local authorities but run by private managers. The Swedish Tourist Board is responsible for site classification and uses the standard system of one to three stars. It is generally recognized that site amenities and cleanliness in Sweden are probably the best in Europe. More than 180 sites fall into the three-star category. Most sites are open from the beginning of June to the end of August; some with winter sports facilities are open throughout the year. Sites tend to be in beautiful countryside, often on a lake or by the sea, but if there is no natural swimming available, swimming pools, either actually on the sites or in the nearest town or village, are always close by. You certainly will not be crowded in on a Swedish camp site as the average pitch size is 80 m (87.5 yd). Camping carnets are usually requested on sites, and if you have not bought one in England, you can obtain the Swedish version, costing about £1, at the first site on which you stay. Sweden is also one of the few countries in Europe where 'camping wild' is allowed. As long as tents are not pitched in the grounds of a house, they can be put up on open land without fear of inter-ference.

It is worth taking a good supply of Camping Gaz as most bottled gas used in Sweden is propane while we use butane. The 904 and 907 Camping Gaz cylinders are available but in limited supplies; the same applies to the gas cartridges.

The most southerly region of Sweden, Skane, is reasonably easy for British holidaymakers to reach. This gently rolling countryside

163

with its sandy beaches and picturesque villages is also *château* country. Further north the coast is more rugged. The west coast, (the port of Gothenburg, the port through which many British visitors enter the country is on this coast) is particularly popular with European holidaymakers. The stretches of long sandy beaches round Helsingborg are safe and very suitable for swimming.

How to get there

Sweden can be approached by direct ferry services operating from Felixstowe or Newcastle to Gothenburg. The crossing takes twenty-three and a half hours. It is also possible to reach Sweden via Denmark, using the Newcastle or Harwich to Esbjerg car-ferry services; sailing time is about nineteen hours. Alternatively, you can take one of the short Channel crossings to France or Belgium, then drive through the Netherlands, northern Germany and Denmark to Sweden, using the Puttgarden–Rodbyhavn and Helsingor–Helsingborg ferry connections. The distance from Calais to Stockholm, the capital, is about 1,600 kilometres (1,000 miles) and would normally require three overnight stops.

Currency and banking

The unit of currency is the Krona divided into 100 öre. Travellers from abroad may import an unlimited sum in foreign banknotes and coins as well as other forms of currency.

In towns, banks are generally open Monday to Friday from 9.30 a.m. to 3.00 p.m., but some may stay open until 6.00 p.m. In the country, banks are usually open from 10.00 a.m. to 2.00 p.m., Monday to Friday.

Medical treatment

UK nationals are entitled to national health benefits to the same extent as a Swedish citizen. Free treatment may be obtained as an in-patient in a public ward of a state hospital. When payment is made for treatment, a receipt should be obtained and produced, together with your passport and any bills for medicine prescribed, at the local administrative office of the district where treatment was obtained. The health insurance office will then refund a proportion of the treatment received. You will have to pay 50 per cent of dental fees.

Public holidays

Holidays based on religious festivals are not always fixed on the calendar but any current diary will give the actual dates. The Whit holiday should not be confused with the British spring bank holiday. The fixed summer holiday is as follows:

1 May Labour Day

In addition, banks are closed all day on Maundy Thursday,

Midsummer Eve (a Midsummer Holiday takes place on the Saturday in the week 20–26 June) and Christmas Eve. Banks and offices close at 1.00 p.m. on the day preceding other public holidays and shops usually close earlier as well.

Shopping hours

Shopping hours vary, especially in large cities, but most shops are open from 9.00 a.m. to 6.00 p.m. from Monday to Friday, and from 9.00 a.m. to 2.00 p.m. on Saturday.

Motoring accidents

It is not necessary to call the police when a motor accident has occurred, but the driver is required to give his or her name and address to other persons concerned, and is not allowed to leave the scene of the accident before this is done, no matter how slight the damage: if he/she does, imprisonment or a fine may result. However, as a general rule, report the matter to the police in your own interest.

Breakdowns

There are alarm centres organized by Larmtjanst AB (Alarm Services Ltd.) or garages which are open day and night to help motorists in difficulties. The service, for which a charge is made, is restricted to breakdowns and accidents.

Drinking and driving

The penalties for driving under the influence of alcohol are extremely severe. If required, the driver must submit to a blood test. According to the amount of alcohol in the blood, the penalty may be a fine or a term of imprisonment.

Lights

Dipped headlights must be used by motorists and motorcyclists during the day throughout the year.

Road conditions

There is a comprehensive network of numbered, well-signposted highways, but minor roads are not numbered. Although many roads in the south are being improved, others – particularly in central and northern Sweden – are still surfaced with loose gravel. There are several stretches of motorway, but these are mainly in the southern part of Sweden.

Protected areas

In various parts of the country, chiefly along the Baltic coast, there are protected areas for animals and plants where only certain roads are open to motorists, and in these areas visitors may stay only at certain places and for a limited time. The two such areas likely to concern visitors are around Boden and Kaux in the province of Norrbotten. Warning notices are displayed in English and other languages on the boundaries of these areas.

NORWAY

The country

Outdoor pursuits such as walking, swimming and sailing are popular in Norway. For walkers there are over twenty mountain areas with specially marked trails and chalets for overnight stops spaced a day's walk apart. As well as sea bathing from the small but numerous beaches, many of them near excellent camp sites, there is good swimming in the Oslo Fjord. For those fond of boating there are plenty of safe, natural anchorages in the creeks and bays of the heavily indented coastline. Details of hiring boats can be obtained from local tourist offices.

There are over 1,300 camp sites in Norway classified by the system of one to three stars. A number of sites provide cabins for campers to use when the weather is bad – a growing practice with practically all the sites north of the Arctic Circle. The cabins are not expensive: equipped with mattresses and cooking facilities they cost between £3.50 and £6 a night. The camping season is short, from mid-June till about the last week in August.

How to get there

Norway can be reached direct by ferry. Services operate from Newcastle to Bergen, Kristiansand, Oslo or Stavanger, or from Harwich to Kristiansand or Oslo. Crossing times vary between seventeen and thirty-one hours, depending on the departure point. Another way of reaching Norway is by using one of the short Channel crossings to France or Belgium, driving through the Netherlands and northern Germany to Denmark, and then either using one of the direct ferry links to southern Norway or travelling via Sweden. The distance from the Channel ports to Oslo via Sweden is about 1,600 kilometres (1,000 miles), and would normally require three overnight stops.

Currency and banking

The unit of currency is the Krone, which is divided into 100 öre. There is no restriction to the amount of Norwegian currency which may be imported, but visitors may be asked to declare all foreign currency, including traveller's cheques, in their possession. There are restrictions on the export of Norwegian money.

Banks are open from 8.15 a.m. to 3.30 p.m. Monday to Friday and are closed on Saturday. Currency may also usually be exchanged at railway stations and airports: their opening hours vary, but are usually 8.00 a.m. to 9.00 p.m. from Monday to Saturday, and 8.00 a.m. to 2.00 p.m. on Sunday. At Bogstad Camping (a well-equipped NAF – Norwegian Motoring Club – site near Oslo) there is an exchange office open from June to August on weekdays with the same opening hours as ordinary banks.

Medical treatment

As there is a British/Norwegian health agreement, no charge is made for in-patient treatment in a public hospital. Reimbursement of about 80 per cent of the cost may be obtained after treatment from a general practitioner, as a hospital out-patient and for certain dental treatment, but prescribed medicines must be paid for. When payment is made, a receipt should be obtained and produced, together with passport, at the social insurance office *(trygdekasse)* of the district where treatment was received. You must claim before you leave Norway.

Public holidays

Holidays based on religious festivals are not always fixed on the calendar but any current diary will give actual dates. The Whit period should not be confused with the British spring bank holiday. Fixed summer holidays are as follows:

1 May   Labour Day
17 May Constitution Day

Shopping hours

Shops are open from Monday to Friday from 8.30 a.m. to 5.00 p.m. and on Saturday from 8.30 a.m. to 2.00 p.m. During the month of July some shops restrict their opening times to 9.00 a.m. to 3.00 p.m.

Motoring accidents

There are no firm rules as to procedure, except where personal injuries are sustained, in which case the police must be called. In such circumstances you should obtain medical assistance for the injured person. It is also advisable to place a warning triangle on the road to notify following traffic of the obstruction.

Breakdowns

The Norwegian Motoring Club (NAF) operates a limited road-patrol service between about 20 June and 1 September. The service operates from 10.00 a.m. to 7.00 p.m. daily, but in view of its limitations a local garage or assistance station may offer to help more quickly. An organization called Viking Redhingstjeneste A/S runs assistance stations but its services are not free.

Drinking and driving

Norwegian law is very strict regarding the consumption of alcohol by drivers. Drivers suspected of being under the influence of drink can be compelled to undergo a blood test; If they are found guilty, their driving licence is taken away and a prison sentence of twenty-one days may be imposed.

Road conditions

In southern and eastern Norway, the main routes have modern surfaces. In the west and north, some road surfaces are oil-bound (partly water-bound) grit. Vehicles with a high ground clearance are more suitable for mountain roads than those with low ground clearance. As a courtesy to other road users, you should fit mudflaps to your car.

In the fjord district, and often in other areas, careful and confident driving is necessary, although gradients are seldom excessive and hairpin bends can usually be easily negotiated. A reasonable touring maximum is 160 to 240 kilometres (100 to 150 miles) a day. This region is mainly unsuitable for large vehicles or caravans. Fjords sometimes have ferry crossings.

Several main roads incorporate stretches of motorway *(motoveg)*. These are mainly around Oslo, with short stretches at Bergen, Stavanger, and Moss. Motorways are divided into two classes: *Motoveg Klasse A*, the usual two-way carriageway; and *Motorveg Klasse B*, the dual carriageway, 6 to 7.5 m (20 to 25 ft) wide and with limited access points.

AUSTRIA
The country
This lovely country, land-locked by six others, has almost as cosmopolitan a life on its camp sites as Spain. There are some four hundred sites in Austria, the majority small, quiet and peaceful. Large sites tend to be near towns, and Vienna revels in the distinction of having more sites on its outskirts than any other European city.

Most sites are open from May to September, with a number remaining open for winter sports. Sites in the popular areas such as the Tyrol and close to the western border tend to become full, particularly at weekends when Germans often nip across for a couple of days camping. At such times campers with an extra spurt of energy could journey further inland.

The Carinthian lake district, a lovely area and important since the twelfth century, has some of Austria's warmest bathing waters. Alan Rogers recommends two sites in this area: Camping Mossler, close to one of the warm lakes, is set in very pleasant surroundings, while Camping Arneitz, said to have exceptionally good sanitary installations, is set directly on the small lake of Faakersee.

Canvas Holidays has a site at the Bavarian end of the Austrian Tyrol. The camp, not far from Reutte, is set in a meadow on the Plansee Lake.

How to get there
The usual approach from Calais, Ostend and Zeebrugge is via Belgium to Aachen to join the German *Autobahn* network, then onwards via Cologne to Frankfurt. Here the routes branch:

southwards via Karlsruhe and Stuttgart for Innsbruck and the Tyrol; or eastwards, via Nürnberg and München, to Salzburg for central Austria. From the Channel ports to Salzburg is about 1,120 kilometres (700 miles), so two overnight stops are needed.

Travelling via the Netherlands is a straightforward run, joining the *Autobahn* system near Arnhem. Alternatively, Austria can be reached via northern France, driving to Strasbourg and Stuttgart or via Basle and northern Switzerland. This is the route to be followed if driving from Dieppe, Le Havre or Cherbourg.

Currency and banking

The unit of currency is the Austrian Schilling, divided into 100 Groschen. There is no restriction on the amount of foreign or Austrian money that may be imported into the country. However, there is a limit to the amount of Austrian money that can be exported; there is no restriction on the export of foreign currency.

Banks are open from Monday to Wednesday and on Friday from 8.00 a.m. to 12.30 p.m., and from 1.30 to 3.00 p.m. On Thursday their hours are 8.00 a.m. to 12.30 p.m. and 1.30 to 5.30 p.m. Exchange offices at some main railway stations are open on Saturdays, Sundays and public holidays.

Medical treatment

In-patient hospital treatment may be free if you show your UK passport. A small charge will be made for dependants. Other medical services must be paid for. There is an emergency medical service; contact the local police if you need to use this.

Public holidays

Holidays based on religious festivals are not always fixed on the calendar but any current diary will give actual dates. The Whit period should not be confused with the British spring bank holiday. Fixed summer holidays are as follows:

1 May	Labour Day
15 August	Feast of the Assumption
26 October	National Holiday

Shopping hours

Shops are generally open from 8.00 a.m. to 6.00 p.m. with a two- to four-hour break around midday. Shops close at noon on Saturdays.

Some shops operate a tax-free service whereby, on leaving the country, visitors are reimbursed for VAT paid. A special form (U34) must be obtained from and completed and stamped by the shop and presented to the Austrian customs when you cross the border. Look for shops displaying the blue 'tax-free shopping' sign or obtain address lists from the local tourist information office.

Motoring accidents

A driver involved in an accident must stop and exchange particulars with the other party. If personal injury is sustained it is obligatory that medical assistance is obtained for the injured people and the accident must be reported to the police. All those who arrive at the scene of an accident are obliged to render assistance, unless it is obvious that everything necessary has been done.

Breakdowns

If your car breaks down, try to move it to the side of the road out of the main flow of traffic and put up a warning triangle behind it. If you need help, telephone the nearest office of the OAMCT (the Osterrichischer-Automobil-Motorrad-und-Touring-Club), the Austrian motoring organization, but expect to be charged for the service.

Compulsory equipment

In Austria all motorists are required by law to carry a first-aid kit and visitors are expected to comply with this regulation. This is not checked at the frontier; however, at the scene of an accident any motorist can be stopped and asked to produce his first-aid kit. If one is not forthcoming, the police may take action.

Drinking and driving

A driver convicted of driving while under the influence of alcohol is severely punished. A fine may be imposed, together with either the withdrawal of the driver's licence or one week's imprisonment. Police are entitled to confiscate the ignition keys of motorists who are apparently under the influence of drink or who are showing signs of exhaustion.

Priority

On mountain roads vehicles travelling uphill have priority. Vehicles which continue straight ahead or make a right-hand turn at a crossroads or intersection have priority over oncoming vehicles turning left, providing that there are no signs to the contrary. In this case even trams cede priority.

A driver wishing to turn across the flow of traffic at a junction controlled by a policeman has to pass in front of him unless otherwise directed.

Road conditions

Austria has a network of well engineered roads. The main traffic artery runs from Bregenz in the west to Vienna in the east via the Arlberg Tunnel, Innsbruck, Salzburg and Linz. Most of the major Alpine roads are excellent, and a comprehensive tour can be made through the Tyrol, Salzkammergut and Carinthia without difficulty. Service stations are fairly frequent, even on mountain roads.

Holiday traffic

In July and August several roads across the frontier become congested, particularly at weekends and on German public holidays. Try to cross the frontier before 10.00 a.m. The crossing points are on the Lindau–Bregenz road at the Brenner Pass (as a possible alternative there is the Resia Pass), at Kufstein, on the München–Salzburg *Autobahn* and on the Villach–Tarvisio road.

SWITZERLAND

The country

There are some 450 camp sites in Switzerland, one of Europe's smallest countries land locked by France, Germany, Austria and Italy. Three hundred and thirty of the country's sites are mentioned in the list issued by the national tourist office. In this list the sites are categorized by numbers, so that a category 3 site has simple installations while a Ia site has specially good facilities. Camp site fees tend to be fairly high: £8 a night for a family of four is an average rather than a ceiling price. However, families with young children score, as there is no charge for those under six, and there are reduced rates for those under twelve.

Swiss camp sites are generally small and, as befits the reputation that this country has for cleanliness, they are well cared for – badly run sites are rare. Summer camping runs from June to August; winter camping, mainly in the sports resorts, from November to May. Canvas Holidays offers rented tents at Lake Thun near Interlaken, while Eurocamp hires them at Lauterbrunnen, also near Interlaken, and at Chatel St Denis near Fribourg.

How to get there

The usual approach from Britain is through France. The distance from the Channel ports to Bern, the capital, is approximately 756 kilometres (470 miles), a journey that would need only one overnight stop.

Currency and banking

The unit of currency is the Swiss franc, which divides into 100 centimes or Rappen. There are no restrictions on the import or export of currency.

Banking hours vary from city to city, so check when you arrive. All banks close on Saturdays. At railway stations in large towns and at airports, exchange offices are open usually from 8.00 a.m. to 8.00 p.m., but these hours may vary in different places.

Medical treatment

There is no free medical treatment for visitors, so it is advisable to have adequate insurance cover for this.

Public holidays

Public holidays based on religious festivals are not always fixed in the calendar, but any current diary will give actual dates. The Whit period should not be confused with the British spring bank holiday. Switzerland has a long list of public holidays varying from canton to canton, even from town to town. Fixed summer holidays are as follows:

19 March Feast of St Joseph
29 June   Feast of St Peter and Paul
15 August Feast of the Assumption

Of the moveable holidays it should be noted that Good Friday is not a holiday in Tessin, while Corpus Christi is celebrated in Roman Catholic areas only.

Shopping hours

In general shops are open from 8.30 a.m. to 6.30 p.m. from Monday to Friday and from 8.30 a.m. to 4.00 p.m. on Saturday. Food stores can however close at 5.30 p.m. on Saturdays in large towns and many are closed on Monday mornings.

Motoring accidents

If any injuries are caused in an accident, the police must be called immediately. It is not necessary to call the police if the accident has caused material damage only. However, the driver must report the incident to the owner of the damaged property and exchange particulars. The police must be informed if this is not possible.

Breakdowns

The major motoring club, the Touring Suisse, operates a patrol service and a day and night breakdown service. This, the Touring Secours, operates from several centres throughout the country and can be called out by telephone. Expect to be charged for this service.

Drinking and driving

A blood test may be required if there is the definite suspicion that a driver is under the influence of alcohol. The penalty when the amount of alcohol in the blood exceeds the permitted amount is either a fine or a prison sentence and the withdrawal of the offender's driving licence for a period of at least two months.

Lights

Driving on sidelights only is prohibited. Spotlights are forbidden. Foglights can be used only in pairs of identical shape, brilliance and colour. Dipped headlights must be used at all times in tunnels, whether they are lit or not: failure to observe this rule can lead to a fine. Switzerland has a special road sign to indicate a tunnel – a red triangle showing a tunnel entrance in the centre – which reminds drivers to turn on dipped headlights. In the open country you must dip your headlights at least 200 m (220 yd) in front of any pedestrian or oncoming vehicle, when you are reversing, travelling in lines of traffic, or stopping. Dipped headlights must be used when waiting at level crossings or near roadwords. They must also be used in badly lit areas when visibility is poor.

Priority
When the road is too narrow for two vehicles to pass, those towing trailers have priority and heavy vehicles have priority over light ones. If two vehicles of the same category cannot pass, the vehicle nearest to the most convenient stopping point or lay-by must reverse. On mountain roads, if there is no room to pass, the descending vehicle must manoeuvre to give way to the ascending one unless the ascending vehicle is obviously near a lay-by. On any stretch of mountain road the driver of a private car may be asked by a postal bus to reverse or otherwise manoeuvre to allow the bus to pass. Postal buses, painted yellow, have a distinctive three-note horn.

If two vehicles are travelling in opposite directions and the driver of each wants to turn left, they must pass in front of each other – not drive round. Drivers turning left may pass in front of traffic islands in the centre of an intersection.

Road conditions
The road surfaces are generally good but some main roads are narrow in places.

Addresses

Freedom of Ryedale Ltd,
23A Market Place,
Helmsley,
North Yorkshire YO6 5BJ.

National Federation of Site Operators,
31 Park Road,
Gloucester GL1 1LH.

South-West Scotland Holiday Parks Association,
Douglas House,
Newton Stewart,
Wigtownshire DG8 6DQ.

The Best of British – 10 camp sites in the scheme:

Blair Castle Caravan Site,
Blair Atholl,
Pitlochry,
Perthshire PH18 5SR.

Brighouse Bay Holiday Park,
Nr Kirkcudbright,
Dumfries & Galloway,
Scotland DG6 4TS.

Graigtoun Meadows Holiday Park,
Mount Melville,
St Andrews,
Fife.

Kennford International Caravan Park,
Exeter,
Devon EX6 7YN.

Mortonhall Caravan Park,
Frogston Road East,
Edinburgh EH16 6TT.

The Orchards Holiday Caravan & Camping Park,
Newbridge,
Isle of Wight.

The Sea View International,
Boswinger,
Gorran Haven,
St Austell,
Cornwall PL26 6LL.

St Helens Caravan Park,
Wykeham,
Scarborough,
North Yorkshire YO13 9QD.

Trevella Park,
Crantock,
Newquay,
Cornwall TR8 5EW.

Wild Rose Caravan & Camping Park,
Ormside,
Nr Appleby,
Cumbria.

7
Emergencies

The best thing about emergencies is that most never happen. The most common ones are dealt with alphabetically in the following pages.

Bites, stings and insect repellents

Most bites and stings suffered in Europe, the majority of them the work of wasps, bees, certain ants and mosquitoes, are annoying rather than dangerous. However, some people are sensitive to stings and can become ill after only one or two: such people will be aware of this tendency and should consult their doctor before going on a camping holiday. For the rest of us, prevention is the best method of protection, and it is therefore wise to take along some sprays and repellents. Wasps can be a particular nuisance on camping holidays, especially at breakfast time when they are attracted by sweet-smelling jams and marmalades. If you want to eat breakfast peacefully outside, use one of the repellents that can safely be left standing on the table and which will not affect food, such as Sectovap, available from chemists and hardware shops at around £1.

There are any amount of insect killing aerosols on the market that can be used to spray inside the tent. Read the can before buying as nowadays they tend to be more specialized, one kind being aimed at wasps and flies, another at ants, and so on.

At lunchtime even the insects seem drowsy and are not too bothersome, but by the evening, the morning wasps will have been replaced by mosquitoes. An effective way to deal with these is to burn Moon Tigers. These, like flat green snakes, are available in packs of six from camp shops and cost around 60p per pack. One placed on the supper table will last all evening.

Ants can be a nuisance on a camping holiday, especially when they climb into food or cool boxes. While sprays are effective, ant powder is perhaps more useful because it is visible and can be placed in a protective ring around any food container standing on the floor.

To stop insects actually landing on your skin, there is a choice of cream, spray or liquid repellents.

If, in spite of all precautions, an insect bite is suffered, dab it with TCP. Vinegar is said to lessen the pain, and calamine lotion too is soothing. Bees sometimes leave their sting behind, and this should be removed as gently as possible so as not to press more venom into the sore. Once the emergency treatment has been applied, an antiseptic cream will help give relief from inflammation, itching or pain. Antisan cream, available in a tube, is reckoned to be effective for insect bites and stings as well as nettle rash and allergic skin reactions. There is also an aerosol, Stingo, which is recommended for insect and fish bites and stings and for plant-produced rashes, which deadens pain, reduces skin temperature and slows down the body's reaction to the venom.

British consulates

There are consular offices in most British embassies in foreign capitals and consulates in some provincial cities. While staff at these offices do all they can to help and advise British subjects in serious difficulties, there are limitations to the services they can provide. They cannot act as social workers, banks, travel agents, employment offices or information bureaux. Neither can they carry out police duties nor give legal advice.

Many consuls are professional or business people who receive no payment for their services, their consularship being purely an honorary appointment. People such as this naturally have to devote the main part of their attention to their business affairs. In larger posts the consul will be a salaried staff member who will deal with requests for assistance.

Call on consuls only in an exceptional emergency. Try to deal by yourself with most emergencies, such as car breakdowns, illness, robbery, shortage of money or accidents. Help is available from a consulate if you are arrested, have lost your passport, or if all prior arrangements to get money to you through private or banking channels have broken down.

If you are arrested, contact, or get someone to contact for you, the nearest embassy, consulate or high commission. The police station should be able to give you the address. The consul cannot intervene in the legal processes of another country but he or she will do all that can properly be done to ensure that you are not discriminated against on nationality or any other grounds and that you receive fair treatment.

For advice about lost or stolen passports, see under the appropriate heading on page 180.

In the case of money not coming through from home to meet the expense of the return journey in an emergency, the consulate will arrange for money to be deposited by relatives or friends with the Foreign and Commonwealth Office in London. All costs or charges that arise out of providing this service will have to be paid for by the holidaymaker. People finding themselves stranded in a foreign country can go to the consul for financial help for the journey home, but not for assistance to enable them to continue their holiday.

An excellent booklet *Essential Information*, which sets out the services available to British subjects in an emergency abroad, is available from the Foreign and Commonwealth Office. Address page 185.

Car breakdown

The first thing to do is to get the car to the side of the road or to a spot where it will not hold up the traffic flow. Put a warning triangle at the appropriate distance behind the car, generally about 30 m (33 yd), and, if the car's electrical system is not at fault, switch on the hazard warning lights. See if you can repair the fault yourself; otherwise look for help. If you are on a motorway, walk to the nearest motorway telephone box to report where the breakdown has happened. Generally these boxes are numbered so the authorities will know your exact position. Otherwise find the nearest garage. If you are a member of a British motoring organization, the AA or the RAC, you could contact the local office of the equivalent motoring organization of the country you are visiting. Depending on the type of insurance policy you have, you may be entitled to some free roadside assistance from one of the main European motoring clubs.

If your car has to be repaired, check, if you are able, that the work has been carried out satisfactorily before paying. In Europe labour and parts can cost more than in the United Kingdom. French garages have to display their charges and when the work is complete give a breakdown on the bill of the charges incurred. Keep all garage receipts and any parts that have been replaced, for they may be needed in an insurance claim.

Some insurance schemes include credit vouchers as part of their package, which can be used to pay for tows, car repairs, medical or legal aid, and so on. If your policy does not include such vouchers and you have to pay for unexpected repairs, it is wise to carry some traveller's cheques in the currency of the country in which you are holidaying.

First-aid box

Most camping shops and chemists sell first-aid boxes, which can cost from as little as £2 to well over £10 each. It is far more satisfactory and far cheaper for each household to make up its own first-aid box. The box should be kept in the car at all times, not just during a holiday, for minor accidents are just as likely to happen on a home picnic as on a continental holiday.

To make a first-aid box, line a clean rectangular biscuit tin or plastic box, about 25 cm × 20 cm and 5 cm deep (10 × 8 in and 2 in deep), with a piece of clean cotton material such as part of an old sheet. Put in a couple of bandages, a packet of gauze or lint, cotton wool for swabs, some TCP or other liquid disinfectant, a tube of cream disinfectant, a roll of sticking plaster and a tin of assorted plasters, a packet of soluble aspirin, anti-diarrhoea pills, laxative tablets, foot powder, calomine lotion (good for soothing bites and stings, as well as sunburn), throat pastilles, scissors, tweezers and a few small safety pins. Everyone will have their own additions to this basic list. Some people, for example, never travel without a thermometer.

It is important that the first-aid box be treated with respect. It should always be kept in the same place in the car or tent, those who have to use it should always wash their hands first, and scissors should not be removed for use in children's cutting-out games.

Medical help

It is as well to read insurance policies before going on holiday to ascertain what kind of cover is provided should illness or accident strike. You should also read two leaflets issued by the Department of Health and Social Security. Leaflet SA36 explains the procedure when dealing with medical charges and reclaiming part or all of the money paid out. Leaflet SA30 tells you how to get medical treatment in EEC and non-EEC countries. It is this leaflet which contains the form CM1 that must be completed to obtain medical treatment in another EEC country.

If medical attention is suddenly needed, get the address of the nearest doctor from camp reception. If it is a bad emergency, ask someone to call an ambulance for you. If you have to attend a doctor's surgery, remember to take a dictionary should you not speak the language. Take the insurance policy along too, as well as the name and telephone number of the broker who issued the policy. You may need to telephone the broker if you have no 'emergency' money and a doctor or hospital is demanding money before giving treatment. If the insurers are satisfied that the claim is valid, they can arrange for the money to be sent in the quickest and most convenient way. Some insurance companies have a representative abroad, and in this case contact him or her rather than the office in the United Kingdom.

Money for emergencies

It is always wise to allow from £50 to £300 'emergency' money when holidaying abroad, even if you just bring it home and re-bank it. At best you might just need it for an unexpected overnight stop in a hotel or for sudden car repair; at worst it may have to be used for medical expenses. Even in countries with which the United Kingdom has a reciprocal health agreement you may find that you have to make a substantial contribution to the cost of hospital care and medicines. Foreign hospitals and doctors may insist on payment of their bills before you leave the country, in other words before you can get home to put in an insurance claim. Be sure to get receipts for all medical treatment you receive. In fact, make a policy of obtaining receipts for all expenses even though you may not need them for insurance purposes. Hotel bills can be useful for reference when you are planning another holiday.

Money: lost or stolen

If you lose or run out of money you can usually draw on the local bank if you have your cheque book and bank card. Look for a bank displaying the Eurocheque sign first, before resorting to an ordinary bank. If you need more money than can be drawn with your bank card (see page 103), you will have to make arrangements for money to be transferred to a bank in the area. To do this, telephone a friend or relative at home and ask them to start the procedure for you. If you do not have a bank account, you can arrange for someone at home to send an international money order, but this takes time.

It is not generally realized that it is not necessary to have a bank account to transfer money through the international banking system to Europe. As long as the sender in Britain is given the name of the bank to which the money has to go, the branch in the town or village as well as the name of the person to whom the money has to be transferred, he or she can go into any branch of any of the main banks in this country with the cash and ask for it to be transferred.

There are three ways of sending money to Europe through a bank. Mail transfer, which takes between seven and ten days, carries a minimum handling charge of £3 and rises to a maximum £25. By this system it costs £2.50 to transfer each £1,000. The second method is by telegraph. This takes about three days and carries a minimum charge of £7, the basic £3 charge plus an additional £4 for the cable. The third way is for the home bank to issue a foreign draft in the currency of the country to which the money has to be sent. This is given to the person handling the negotiations in Britain and is posted by him or her to the person abroad. Again, there is a £3 handling charge.

If traveller's cheques are lost or stolen, their disappearance must be reported to the police. Do not forget to make a note of the numbers of traveller's cheques as this will speed up the refund service should they go missing. When you are issued with the cheques you will be given a booklet listing the names of agents authorized to make repayments up to a certain value if the cheques are lost or stolen.

Passports: lost or stolen

If passports disappear on the camp site, first ask at reception whether they have been handed in. If not, go immediately to the police and subsequently to the British consulate in the area. If your passport is not handed in, the consulate is empowered to issue an emergency passport, for a fee, to enable you to return home if you are not allowed to leave the country without a passport. Expect to be delayed while enquiries are made about the loss of the passport and before a temporary one can be issued. As with other important documents, it is as well to keep a note of your passport number and the date and place of issue separately from the passport itself.

Poste restante

If you are camping with a rent-a-tent company you will be able to leave a precise address with relatives or friends at home. If you plan to move around with your own equipment but have an approximate idea of when you will be near certain towns you can arrange to collect letters at the main post office. People writing to you will simply put your name, then Post Restante, the name of the town followed by the name of the country on the envelope. In Italy *Fermo in Posta* is used instead of post restante and *Lista de Correos* in Spain.

To collect mail you will need to take your passport along to the post office as a means of identification. Postal and delivery times vary throughout Europe so do not be too precise about times of arrival of letters from the United Kingdom, plan a stay of between four days to a week in an area if you are expecting mail at the main post office.

Robbery

Any robbery should be reported immediately to the local police. If you intend to submit an insurance claim when you get home, be sure to get a copy of the report you hand over to the police listing the stolen goods.

Storms

Tents are far more vulnerable to bad weather than houses. Never trust the weather and never make the mistake of leaving chairs, tables or swimming costumes outside at night because you are convinced it will not rain during the hours of darkness – it invariably does. Remember too that heavy dews can make chairs too damp to use for breakfast and swimming gear unpleasantly clammy for that early morning swim.

If a really bad storm is forecast, it pays to take certain precautions. First, make sure that nothing inside the tent is pressing against the canvas: pressure points will cause the rain to seep through. Check that all storm flaps over windows have been rolled down and secured. Slacken off guy ropes to allow for any canvas shrinkage that might occur if the tent gets very wet.

Some people dig a trench round the tent to drain away water that may accumulate in a particularly heavy downpour. There are two schools of thought on this practice: some campers think it a very proper course of action, particularly in areas renowned for their sudden, short, sharp and heavy rain storms; others feel that trench digging is not really necessary, that it spoils the pitch – not everyone may want to put their tent up in the patch marked out by the trench – and that it is not always effective. If you are a committed 'trencher', carry a narrow, pointed spade: these sudden rain storms seem to occur in the Mediterranean where the ground is hard and stony. Collapsible shovels for campers cost between £3 and £10. They can be useful snow shovels if kept in the car during the winter.

If strong winds as well as heavy rain are predicted, it is as well to know about a practice called 'storm lashing'. In ten years of camping I have never had to put it into operation – it is probably a practice that applies more to single tents pitched in high places than to family tents. Storm lashing involves pegging extra guy ropes from side to side across the tent to prevent the canvas from billowing out when the wind is high and to lessen the strain on the pegs.

Another method of protecting the tent against high winds is to use storm props. These are additional poles that stretch diagonally across the tent, bracing the whole structure in a high wind and so making it firm and stable. It can be most alarming when the tent starts swaying from side to side as the wind rises. Storm props are available from camping shops and can be extended to fit most width of tent. They cost around £5 each.

Sunburn

Fair British skins are not made for roasting, so take care and do not

181

overdo the sunbathing, even when camping at home. Take special care of young children in Mediterranean countries: all those stories about the intensity of the midday sun are true. Even continental families pack up and leave the beach to rest in the shade at lunch-time. Many beaches empty at around midday with often only the foolhardy British staying on, brilliant red in the sun.

One of the hazards of sunburn is that it does not show instantly and people are inclined to stay in the sun longer than they should. It really is best for adults to stick to the rule of between ten and fifteen minutes a side for sunbathing. As for children who run round rather than lie in the sun, the rule is to watch their shoulders and backs, especially when they are crouched down playing at the water's edge. They should put on a T-shirt after the first ten minutes or so of play. Watch too for sunburn weals round the close-fitting legs of swimming trunks and bathing costumes. Swimming gear with loose-fitting legs is best for Mediterranean holidays.

Apart from the fact that too much sun ages the skin, there is the threat of skin cancer after prolonged exposure. Dermatologists are still debating as to whether two of the ingredients used in certain sun filters can lead to an increased risk of skin cancer. Manufacturers claim that filters containing psoralen or bergamot oil, the two ingredients in question, help rapid tanning and so build up a protection against the sun. Some years ago skin specialists were advising holidaymakers to buy creams that did not contain psoralen, so check labels for contents before buying.

A very small number of people can develop an allergic rash to sun creams. If this happens, swap to another brand,. Best of all, try the cream before going on holiday. Put some test patches on an exposed arm or leg and wait to see if a rash develops during the day. If it does not, and in most cases it will not, the cream is safe for you and you can stock up.

If anyone does overdo the sunbathing and starts to suffer from heat exhaustion, they will need plenty of fluids and rest in a cool place. The symptoms of heat exhaustion, which can precede mild sunstroke, are light-headedness, dizziness when moving around, fatigue and nausea. So be warned by these early symptoms. In serious cases of heatstroke the temperature can rise quite high and the patient may lose consciousness. If this happens, send for a doctor and wrap the patient up in a wet sheet to reduce the temperature. Nothing as dramatic or alarming as this will occur if you treat the sun with caution. Sunstroke is more likely to happen when groups of youngsters go off camping on their own, often in sites without any shade.

Telephones

Telephoning home from Europe has certainly become a good deal easier in the past few years since the introduction of international codes and coin-box kiosks have made it possible to do the job oneself without having to go through the lengthy and often expensive business of getting either a hotel receptionist or an official in a post office to make the call. There are still some places, generally in country areas away from towns and cities, where there are no coin-box kiosks. If you do not relish the thought of having to make a telephone call through a third person, you should plan ahead and make telephone calls when you can use a kiosk.

Make sure that you know the international dialling code for your number at home – it is not always the same as the local code. Check that you have the right code for friends and relatives you may want to ring. Carry with you the complete telephone number of the broker who issued your insurance policy: in an emergency, say when money has to be forwarded quickly to meet a hospital bill, you may need to contact him/her or the insurance company quickly. Always have to hand the telephone number of the port from which you intend to cross back to Britain, in case you want to change your journey time. Many ferry companies give the addresses and telephone numbers of ports on the tickets, but always check this. It is frustrating and time-wasting to drive all the way to the port only to find the crossing you had hoped to change to is full. It is always easier for passengers without cars to transfer to another sailing: ferries can accommodate far more passengers than they can cars.

Nowadays most European telephone kiosks have visual as well as verbal explanations of how to make international calls, so you need not necessarily understand the language; but take a dictionary along in case there are complications. The Post Office has issued a series of good information leaflets entitled *Phoning and Writing Home*. There are four leaflets in the series for Europe: one covers France, Belgium, the Netherlands and Luxembourg; one is for Austria, Switzerland and the Federal Republic of Germany; one is for Cyprus, Greece, Italy, Malta, Morocco, Portugal, Spain and Yugoslavia; and one covers Denmark, Finland, Norway and Sweden. People camping with rent-a-tent companies will probably receive the appropriate leaflet in their pack; independent campers should telephone 100 and ask for freephone 2013 (the number is the same all over Britain) to request the leaflet they require. As well as giving detailed information on how to telephone home, what coins to use, how to understand the signals and how to identify continental boxes, the leaflets also list postage rates for letters and postcards destined for home and indicate where stamps can be bought other than at a post office.

Upset stomachs

By far the most common holiday complaint is an upset stomach. Some cases of food poisoning can be quite serious, but the majority of holidaymakers suffer a mild attack and do not require outside medical attention.

Most holiday stomach disorders result from eating contaminated food or drinking impure water. Campers in Britain, being self-caterers, can avoid most of the hazards by observing the normal rules of hygiene followed at home. Always wash hands before preparing or cooking food, wash fruit and vegetables that are to be eaten raw, and be wary of using food that has been cooked one day and kept unrefrigerated overnight. In fact, try to avoid using left-overs when the weather is anything other than cool, however much it goes against your natural instinct not to waste food.

The risk of food poisoning increases once the Channel is crossed and is greatest in countries where the public health requirements leave much to be desired. It has been estimated that one in five travellers to southern Europe is stricken by some form of upset stomach. When camping abroad, therefore, it is wise to augment the basic hygiene rules which you follow at home. As an extra precaution always peel fruit and vegetables to be eaten raw; if doubtful about the supply, boil milk; and if the family has a meal out choose well-cooked meat and avoid those well-known hazards of shell fish and ice cream unless you know you are in a restaurant you can trust. Even ice cubes can be a source of infection if the water supply is contaminated, so avoid these too.

When camping abroad always be sure to draw drinking water from the right tap, which should be clearly marked. If in doubt, ask.

Take medicines along in case anyone is stricken. The World Health Organization has devised a drink for sufferers. The ingredients of the mixture are based on the essential nutrients lost during the illness: fluids, minerals and glucose all have to be replaced. These are put together in a drink by adding a pinch of salt and a teaspoon of either sugar or honey to fruit juice (not squash) and topping it up with fizzy mineral or soda water. Drink this two or three times a day with plenty of other liquids and you should be well on the road to recovery. It is as well to stick to bottled water rather than tap water during this period. Sufferers should rest as much as possible and keep out of the sun; adults should avoid drinking alcohol. If the symptoms persist after two or three days, consult the local doctor. When the infection has passed, keep away from raw fruit and vegetables for a couple of days and go easy on milk and alcohol. Some people find that, if they can keep it down, eating plenty of bread in the early stages helps to absorb the poison.

Water supply

Anyone camping in a country where there may be doubt about the water supply should take along purifying tablets. These are available from chemists and camping shops. Usually they are dissolved in water which has to stand for thirty minutes before being used. Wash vegetables in sterilized water if the supply is impure. Tea and coffee made from sterilized water tastes quite normal.

Finally, some aids to survival. Survival Aids Ltd specializes in stocking items that are needed in emergencies, such as a wide range of water-purifying agents, emergency rations, waterproof torches, insect creams and even shark repellent. Send 50p for a copy of their catalogue.

The St John Ambulance Brigade has produced a free ten-page booklet, *First Aid in an Emergency*, that can be slipped inside the first-aid box. As its name implies, it explains, with the aid of illustrations, how to cope with nine of the most common accidents: choking, electrical injury, external bleeding, nosebleeds, fainting, sprains, fractures, burns and scalds and foreign bodies lodged in the eye. If the local branch is unable to supply a copy, one can be obtained from the organization's London headquarters.

Addresses

Foreign and Commonwealth Office,
Clive House,
Petty France,
London SW1H 9HD.

St John Ambulance HQ,
1 Grosvenor Crescent,
London SW1X 7F.

Survival Aids Ltd,
Morland,
Penrith,
Cumbria CA10 3AZ.

Bibliography

Finally, whether camping in Great Britain or Europe there are some practical books worth taking along.

Nature books

For those interested in wild flowers there are two beautifully illustrated books. *The Alpine Flowers of Great Britain and Europe* by Marjorie Blamey and Christopher Grey-Wilson and *The Wild Flowers of Britain and Northern Europe* by Marjorie Blamey, Richard Fitter and Alastair Fitter, both published by Collins cost around £4.50 each. They are so comprehensive as surely to count as definitive works, certainly for the amateur. There are also good family reference books on birds, rocks and minerals in the same series. Other publishers produce similar well-illustrated reference books.

Guide to the Gardens of Britain and Europe by Elizabeth Drury and Harriet Bridgeman, published by Granada at £3.50, is a paperback covering twenty-two countries. As well as a brief description of the contents of over 1,000 gardens open to the public there are site location maps, always important, and a short historical perspective which is helpful.

A book to interest gardeners on holiday in this country is *Green Pages* by Veronica Crichton and Maud Crawford, published by Granada at £3.95. This, the only guide of its kind to the nurseries and garden centres of the British Isles, has over 1,000 entries. Gardeners looking for unusual specimens will find the list of 'plant sources' helpful. Names and addresses of nurseries that supply all manner of plants, from trees to bulbs are given. Once again there is a location map, and the name of the owner of each nursery is given as well as opening times and a description of the stock.

Houses

Those who enjoy historic houses should find the *Historic Houses, Castles and Gardens in Great Britain & Ireland*, published by ABC Publications at £1.50, enormously helpful. This annual 'bible' lists most of the habitable properties open to the public, including those that open very infrequently or by appointment only. The book includes many buildings that have changed very little and have not been spruced up especially for visitors, places such as Hellen's at Much Marcle in Herefordshire, where the Black Prince dined, and which still has much of the original furnishings. Careful reading of this book will turn up gems all over the country. Good practical information on how to reach the houses is included as well as opening times and charges. If ordered from the publishers the book costs £2.30, including postage and packing.

Stately Homes, Museums, Castles & Gardens in Britain, published by the AA at £2.75, extends the net even wider as it includes wildlife parks, zoos and museums. A very good book for family holidays at home, particularly for days when the weather is not so good.

A Handbook of European Architectural Styles, by Wilfried Koch, published by Foulsham at £2.95, is excellent. Do not be put off by the title, this book is far from stuffy. It is readable and informative with plenty of lovely little drawings: just the thing for home or abroad.

Cookery books

Shopping and cooking in Europe by Nicholas Courtney, published by Hutchinson in paperback at £3.95, very sensibly takes readers round the markets of Europe, gives shopping vocabulary and, where necessary, descriptions of food. The recipes, listed under countries, are imaginative, and many can be used by campers.

There are instructions for cooking artichokes and preparing *moules marinières*, both very simple but dishes which perhaps many people would not attempt on holiday.

Cook out by Frances Kitchen, published by David and Charles at £3.95, is aimed at the hungry family camping in England and includes recipes for such filling dishes as boiled beef and carrots, hot boiled bacon and such traditional English puddings as jellied trifle and steam pudding. If this sounds a bit too familiar, there is a useful section on pressure cooking for the camper. There is also an informative section on English wild herbs and flavourings, edible berries, nuts and fungi and an explanation of English regional dishes.

Leisure Cookery, by Valerie Taylor, published by Rougemont Publications at £1.25, is also aimed mainly at the camper in Britain, with recipes given for such dishes as mince and rice, meat loaf, braised steak and various ways of cooking pork chops. However, there are pressure cooker recipes and others, quick and easy, that sound simple enough for camping.

Picnic by Claudia Roden, published by Jill Norman at £8.50, has a good practical chapter, 'Cooking in the Open', which gives a great deal of advice on barbecues, including the various types of wood to use.

Barbecue Cookbook, by Mary Berry, published in paperback by Martyn Books at £1.25, gives practical advice on barbecues, from how to build them to how to get the best out of them and how to clean them. The recipes, not too complicated, are backed by information on bastes, sauces and marinades, and rounded off by a section on soups, salads, vegetables and a few simple puddings.

Guide Books

The Berlitz travel guides to most European countries, about £1.25 each, and the Collins *Welcome to* books, £1.95 each, covering countries and capital cities, are good value and full of practical information, vocabulary and maps and, in the case of the Collins books, town plans of some of the major cities. Excellent and comprehensive guides to individual countries are produced by Michelin, £3.50 each, Fodor, £5.50 each, and Baedeker's travel guides, produced in conjunction with the AA, £5.95 each. A pocket-sized dictionary is always worth including in the camping library.

Index

Page numbers in bold refer to the address of an organization.